COVERING HOME

# COVERING HOME

*Lessons on the Art*
*of* FATHERING *from the Game*
*of* BASEBALL

## JACK PETRASH

**Robins Lane Press**
*a division of Gryphon House, Inc.*
BELTSVILLE, MARYLAND

Library of Congress Cataloging-in-Publication Data

Petrash, Jack, 1949–
     Covering Home : lessons on the art of fathering from the game of baseball /
     Jack Petrash.
          p. cm.
     Includes bibliographical references and index.
     ISBN 0-87659-217-5
     1. Fatherhood. 2. Father and child. 3. Baseball. I. Title.

     HQ756.P475 2000
     306.874'2—dc21

                                                                    00-060975

The following excerpts have been reprinted by permission:

*Bird by Bird* by Anne Lamott, Reprinted by permission of Random House.

*Memories of Summer* by Roger Kahn, Reprinted by permission of Hyperion.

*Wait Till Next Year* by Doris Kearns Goodwin, Reprinted by permission
     of Simon & Schuster.

*Fathering* by Will Glennon, Reprinted by permission of Conari Press.

*Manhood: An Action Plan for Changing Men's Lives* (2nd Edition) by Steve Biddulph,
     Reprinted with permission of Finch Publishing, Australia.

*Education of the Child & Early Lectures in Education* by Rudolf Steiner, Reprinted
     by permission of Anthroposophic Press.

*Youth Longs to Know* by John F. Gardner, Reprinted by permission
     of Anthroposophic Press.

*Turning,* Anonymous, Reprinted by permission of Anthroposophic Press.

Book design by Katherine Thomason, Charles Nix & Associates.

# CONTENTS

# Contents

*To my children, Jonathan, Josh, and Ava,*
*the heart of the order.*

*To my wife, Carol, simply for being here.*

*To my dad, for teaching me to hit left-*
*handed because it was only 296 feet down*
*the right field line in Yankee Stadium,*
*and for so much more.*

At a recent National Summit on Fathering in Washington, D.C., Wade Horn, president of the National Fatherhood Initiative, showed a video of a public service advertisement that his organization had produced for distribution on national television and that was designed to encourage fathers to play an active role in the lives of their children. This short segment opens with a scene reminiscent of the Robert Redford movie *The Natural*. A young boy is standing in an open, sunlit meadow holding a baseball glove and a ball. The action moves in slow motion as the boy winds up and throws the ball. The camera follows the flight of the ball through the air, but to the viewer's surprise it lands in the grass and rolls to a stop. The boy runs after the ball, picks it up, winds up, and throws it back the other way. Again, there is no one there to catch it. A voice then says, "Four out of ten children in America grow up in a home without a father."

The simple act of playing catch was one of my most commonly shared activities with my father. In fact, when I was young, baseball was almost always a part of what we did together or talked about. My dad gave me my first glove, my first bat, and my first baseball book (the *'56 Yankees Yearbook*), and he took me to my first game. He helped me to decipher the strange hieroglyphics of the box score and with discreet comments introduced me to the mysteries of the game, such as the inexplicable fact that the player who makes a great play to end an inning often leads off when his team comes to bat.

Of course, there were things that my father did not tell me about baseball; some aspects of this game are far older than Abner Doubleday. According to the Oriental Institute at the University of Chicago, the pharaoh in ancient Egypt had a religious ritual in which he would hit a leather-covered sphere with a stick to the temple priests. The priests would catch the ball and by doing so "gladden the heart" of the goddesses Sekhmet and Hathor. Both of these goddesses obviously knew the importance of good defense. Although my father didn't tell me about this aspect of its history, he did let me know that the game of baseball was special, perhaps more special than any of us suspected.

So it was no wonder that I wanted baseball to be something I shared with my children. As my sons came of age, I supplied myself with a catcher's mitt and *The Baseball Encyclopedia* and found baseball an easy way to connect with them. When my daughter was born, I never thought our relationship needed to be different. She visited the National Baseball Hall of Fame (*in utero*) and attended her brothers' games as an infant, a toddler, and a young girl. When she went to her first major league baseball game, it was love at first sight. Pitcher Scott Kamieniecki handed her a carnation as she came through the turnstile, and then Ken Griffey, Jr., hit a line drive into the stands that we caught.

But this book, *Covering Home*, is about more than just connecting with our children via baseball. It is also about seeing how the lessons that baseball teaches us can be applied to fathering. There is a place in us where our passionate commitments converge, and it is there that fathering and baseball intertwine. The lessons that I have learned in one have instructed me in the other, how in fathering as in baseball you have to work on fundamentals, develop good habits, avoid errors, work on your control, and always keep in mind that you can't win them all.

*Covering Home* is part spring training, part team meeting, and part clinic. It focuses on fundamental aspects of good fathering and tries to address particular situations that may be symptomatic of problems. Its purpose is to assist fathers. My conversations with fathers have shown me repeatedly that they want to do a good job. They are committed to their children and the process of parenting, and because of changing gender roles, they are often assuming more parenting responsibility than their own fathers or grandfathers.

Fatherhood has changed significantly in recent years, and the fathers I have spoken with are continually finding themselves in new parenting situations. In the busyness of modern times where both parents work and travel and go back to school, fathers are repeatedly covering home. Knowing when to cover home is essential. It requires knowledge of what should happen in a given situation but also an awareness of what could go wrong. Whether it's an overthrow, a passed ball, a snow day, or a sick child, we need to be alert, as well as ready and willing to act.

The stories and experiences that appear in this book have come to me in a number of ways over the past twenty-eight years. During that time I have been both a parent and a teacher. As a parent I have raised three children, two sons and a daughter, and needless to say, they have taught me so much. Many of the comments on what *not* to do in certain situations have been learned the hard way.

I also learned a great deal about children and fathers from being a teacher. At the Washington Waldorf School in Bethesda, Maryland, I was assigned as the primary teacher for the same group of children for eight years. I started as their first-grade teacher and stayed with the same students until the end of eighth grade. Doing this with three groups of children over a span of twenty-four years gave me a rich experience of child development and allowed me to know young children and teenagers equally well. It also enabled me to become an extended member of my students' families. This helped me to see many different parenting styles and to have extensive and prolonged contact with many fathers. As I watched, I learned from other men how to be a better father and at the same time developed a sense of the unique features of fatherhood. It was also through my conversations with these men, through their stories and their insights, that clear patterns began to emerge. These are the understandings that I have tried to convey through these lessons on the art of fathering.

It is my hope that *Covering Home* will assist and empower fathers who are eager to play a significant role in the lives of their children and who have a heartfelt affection for the game of baseball. But it is also my wish that this book will serve those dads who simply have a deep and abiding love for their children and a desire to be the best fathers possible.

## IF YOU WANT THE SEASON
## OF A LIFETIME, PREPARE FOR IT

♦

WITHOUT SPRING TRAINING, THE FIRST
HALF OF A BASEBALL SEASON WOULD BE A
CALAMITY OF WALKS, STRIKEOUTS, AND
ERRORS. TAKE THE TIME TO WORK ON FUN-
DAMENTALS; UNDERSTAND YOUR ROLE AS
A FATHER AND CULTIVATE A WILLINGNESS
TO CHANGE YOURSELF FOR THE GOOD OF
YOUR CHILD.

*I know of no more encouraging fact than*
*the unquestionable ability of man to elevate*
*his life by conscious endeavor.*

—HENRY DAVID THOREAU

This summer I was walking behind a father and his son on the
way to the beach. The father was a young man in his thirties and
the little boy was around four. The boy was holding his father's
hand, looking up at him as they walked, and asking him questions that I couldn't help but overhear. "Do you like me, Daddy?"
the little boy asked. "Of course, I like you," the father replied. "I
don't like you, Daddy," the boy responded. I hesitated, feeling
that I should not be privy to this conversation. Then after a prolonged pause, the little boy repeated, "I don't like you, Daddy. I
love you."

This story doesn't end here. As I looked closely at these two,
I noticed that below the father's baseball cap his hair had an

uneven quality because clumps of it were missing and his scalp was showing through. Later that day on the beach, I saw the father again. He had his shirt off and I could see a large red scar down the center of his abdomen from a recent surgery. This father knew too well what healthy fathers can so easily forget: Being a father is a precious opportunity.

Wanting to make the most of this precious opportunity could lead you to ask "How do I prepare myself to be a good father?" You could be a man who is seriously thinking ahead to what it will take if and when you and your wife decide to become parents. Or you could be one of the many men who has been surprised and slightly stunned by the statement "We are pregnant." Perhaps you are already a father, maybe a father of more than one child, or a single father. And even though everything is going reasonably well, your parenting has become routine and lethargy has settled in. You sense that your fathering needs to regain its vitality and focus.

It is also possible that you are a father who has just had one of those disastrous days that we all have, a day when we demonstrate the uncanny ability to do and say the wrong thing at the wrong time and to act in a way that we swore we never would. If that is the case and the reason that you are now opening this book, take heart. You probably have the most important requirement for being a good father: a willingness to change.

This is a primary way in which baseball and fathering are similar. We start out as rookies with ample portions of problems and promises. Early on we have holes in our swing or a propensity for giving up long home runs, but we also have moments of brilliance. Minimizing weaknesses and maximizing brilliance is the work of player development. Back in the early seventies, the Kansas City Royals had a baseball academy in Florida for this very reason. It was there that they groomed Willie Wilson, Frank White, and future Hall of Fame member George Brett.

Like baseball, fathering is a path of development. It will not allow us to be the same people in the end that we were at the beginning. Through repeated practice and repeated gaffes, fatherhood will enable us to develop admirable qualities such as self-sacrifice, restraint, perseverance, flexibility, and more. These qualities will either develop with our conscious assistance or in spite of our unconscious reluctance. But if we are fathers in the true sense of the word, they will develop. Fatherhood will call on us to grow in ways that we never imagined.

Self-development can take place at different speeds and on different levels. There are quick changes that occur on a superficial level. These readily noticeable changes involve alterations in thoughts and ideas. These changes come quickly, but they just begin to scratch the surface. Their value is limited; it is simply too easy to talk a good game. Slow change is what we're after, and it occurs on a deeper level. It is the breaking of long-held habits. These changes go unnoticed as we go about our business and then, after much work, we are surprised one day to see that we are different. We have taken our game to the next level. This is the opportunity that fatherhood presents to us. It gives us the chance to develop in a deeply significant way. To effect this change, fatherhood will place demands on us. It will ask that we bring the same intensity and focus to parenting as we bring to our most serious endeavors. And it will ask for our best on three distinct levels, through our *active participation*, *emotional involvement*, and *conscious and thoughtful awareness*.

One example of how we need to prepare ourselves is in the transition from work to home. When you have already given your best for eight or ten hours, it is difficult to have more to give. Our best forces of heart and mind have been intensely engaged during the day, and now as we arrive home we try to separate ourselves from work consciousness and turn our attention to the home. Often, this is not easy to do.

The Baltimore Orioles, the closest thing Washington, D.C., has to a local baseball team, had a unique outfielder back in the late seventies. His name was Ken Singleton, and he had an unusual habit when he came to bat that worked quite well for him. Whenever he stepped into the batter's box, he would reach down and pick up three pebbles. This was his disciplined routine, and he did it without fail. These pebbles were a reminder that each time he batted, he was entitled to three good pitches. This consciously repeated act heightened his awareness and increased his discipline and patience as a hitter by keeping him from being overanxious. Whenever I heard the radio announcers mention this ritual, I always thought of it as a practice from an imaginary book called *Zen and the Art of Hitting*.

I think that fathers need a similar ritual. We should stop outside the door when we are about to make the transition to our children's world and imagine that we are about to pick up one, two, or three stones, depending on the number of hours we will have with our children before their bedtime. At this moment we should remind ourselves that we are going to spend these hours with the most important people in the world.

The fact is that our children grow up far too quickly. Before most of us are ready, our children's focus will shift and we will no longer be the center of their attention. In fact, in all too short a time, they will be out the door and on their own. If we care about the relationship we have with our children, these evening hours are critical. This is when a large portion of the real parenting work happens. This is when we need to begin to meet our children in three fundamental ways—actively, emotionally, and thoughtfully.

Roger Kahn's book *Memories of Summer* contains an interview with Willie Mays that sheds light on these three aspects. Mays is discussing what it takes to be a great ballplayer:

> So much is mental. I believe if you can't think, you can't play [on a good level]. Baseball or any other sport. People don't appreciate this enough....
>
> Some people who watched Jim Brown play football said, "Man, he's big and fast and strong. He's gotta be good." But they don't realize that when Brown was running with the ball, he was always thinking ahead, two or three moves ahead of the tacklers....
>
> Muhammad Ali. Sure he was big and quick. But he was such a good boxing thinker. He could figure the round he'd win in before the fight. Then he made his moves and it would come out like he predicted. He was another athlete [who was] great because he would think.... Julius Erving in basketball. Dr J. had all the moves. He had a great body to play basketball, but he had the moves because he knew how to think.
>
> ...and I see something else with Michael [Jordan]. You remember long ago I told you, a player has to love the game. I look at Michael and I see a player who loves basketball. He loves playing it the way I loved playing baseball. Intelligence, sure, but love is a big reason Michael can play basketball the way he does.

To be a great ballplayer or any sort of great athlete, you need more than just physical ability. You also need keen mental awareness and a deep emotional involvement. These are the same three key components of great fathering.

## ACTIVELY INVOLVED

The obvious starting point for engaging in the game of baseball is active participation. We must be physically present in all the daily routines and rituals. Batting practice, fielding practice, calisthenics, running, and stretching require our complete active involvement. Fathering places the same demands on us.

Picture a father arriving home after a long day at work. He opens the door to the house and is greeted by a flurry of activity. The warmth and familiarity of the home are comforting, and inwardly the father breathes a sigh of relief. After being "on" all day, he is glad to be "off." But at the same time he is exhausted from the long day at work and drained from the rush-hour commute. He exchanges greetings, changes his clothes, and begins to decompress. As he makes his way past the living room he is drawn to the couch. Tonight, he is eager just to sit down, if only for a moment.

As he sinks into the soft cushions of the couch he reaches for the remote control and gives himself over, if only briefly, to the world of the evening news. Instantly he is engrossed, but this will not last. Before the father has noticed, the children have drawn near. Soon they are underfoot, up on the chair, and crawling across his lap. "Daddy, Daddy" is their incessant cry.

Here is the first opportunity for growth. The children are desperately seeking an active father. They are searching for some signs of animated life from the man whose face is illumined in a pale blue light and who neither moves nor speaks. The children long for their father to get up, to do or say something, at the very least just to sit up and respond.

It is only a recent historical development that fathers are not active around the home. For the great expanse of human history, men worked at home. They tilled and herded; they built and repaired. Since the Industrial Revolution, it has become the custom that fathers work outside the home, thereby denying children an experience for which they long, to observe firsthand their father's active and purposeful working.

Our children long for us to do things in their presence. Most fathers are unaware how important even the simplest actions can be. The way we take off our shoes and hang our coat, the way we store our tools or open our briefcase, all make a lasting impression on our children. Even the objects associated with our work—our toolbox, our computer, our legal pads and stationery—have power and appeal. If we think back to our own early childhood, we will recall how much we admired what our fathers could do when we were young and not yet able.

Children long to be active just like their parents. They want to learn how to do all that they see us and others do. At some point it will probably fall to us to teach our children how to ride a bike, drive a car, row a boat, or use a saw. Our active involvement will have an added dimension; it will be an educational experience. All that we do in our children's presence is instructive, more instructive than most of us realize.

Being active, however, is not the easiest task, particularly after a hard day's work. It is especially difficult for fathers to shift from the activities of the work environment to the activities of home. Whether we are coming directly home or picking up our children from daycare or a friend's house, some inner adjustment is necessary. It takes us a while to adjust to a child's world, a world that has a different sense of time and sometimes no apparent sense of order and organization. We need to be ready when we enter the home because this is a pivotal moment in the day for everyone in our family.

## EMOTIONALLY INVOLVED

Since my sons were in high school, I have been a coach at our school. On a number of occasions, I have had serious high school ballplayers turn to me on a spring day, either at practice or after a game, and simply say, " I love this game." This was the same feeling that prompted the great baseball enthusiast and Hall of Fame shortstop Ernie Banks to say, "Let's play two today." When we participate with strong emotional focus, we belong to the game and it is obvious that we care. This is the same heartfelt way that fathers need to meet their children.

Being emotionally accessible to our children, however, is often difficult for dads. This is partly because we are not accustomed to relating in this way, nor is it encouraged in the workplace. It is also because many of us did not have the experience of seeing our own fathers relate on an emotional level when we were young, and so we lack models for this type of behavior.

In speaking with other dads, I discovered that it was not uncommon for our own fathers to have come home from work in a state of emotional upset. A bad day on the job could be sensed in an almost physical way. Our father's emotions certainly affected the atmosphere in the home. What we, as fathers, feel helps to create the emotional weather in our home, the weather that our children experience. It was not uncommon for me or my friends to sense the weather change from pleasant to stormy when our fathers came home from work. Our father's inner life could be swirling with the events of the day and all we would be told was, "Leave your father alone. He's had a hard day." We were left to make sense of our father's moods without guidance. When we became parents we had no choice but to set off in a new direction, knowing only that we didn't want to go that way.

This is another example of how important the transition is from work to home. It is essential that we not enter our homes encumbered by the cares of the day. We need to free ourselves from the day's experiences so that our emotional activity can focus on our family.

A friend of mine runs his own auto body shop, a very successful business with a large staff and an excessive amount of insurance-related paperwork. He spends his day in demanding, but enjoyable, work. When work is over, he has this ritual before heading for home: He pulls his car into one of the bays and washes it, whether it needs it or not. With the only sound being that of the hose, with the feel of the water on his hands, with the large rhythmical sweep of his arm as the towel moves across the hood and the fenders, he wipes away the tensions of the day. Purposeful physical activity can be the perfect remedy for the stress and nervousness that are often by-products of our busy lives. To be ready to be emotionally involved at home, a father needs to begin preparation even before he reaches the door.

Emotional involvement is harder to describe than physical activity. It is an inner activity and therefore more elusive. Yet our emotional activity is of great importance to our children. They learn to assess it in our features. They are sensitive to it in our tone of voice. They find it hidden in a casual and seemingly innocuous remark. What we feel and *that* we feel matters to our children.

Perhaps the best way to understand the essentials of emotional involvement is to picture a past relationship, one when you were young and very much in love. Think of the way that you listened then, as if every word conveyed some special meaning. Think of the way that you observed so many details: gestures, facial expressions, a characteristic posture. It was as if observation itself were a sensual pleasure and each perception revealed to you a secret about the person you loved.

Now it may be hard to duplicate that kind of emotionally charged observation. And yet it provides the starting point for our emotional involvement with our children—a quiet, sympathetic, yet active, watching and listening to all that our children do and say so that we can uncover some glimpse of who they are. It is certainly how they watch us.

Emotional involvement also means finding physical ways to be expressive. Some dads are good at this. I admire fathers who are able to show their affection for their children through a spontaneous physical embrace, to effortlessly draw their children up on their lap, to put an arm around them, and to kiss them good-bye whenever they leave. To physically express our affection is important. Those fathers who can do this with ease have a great gift; it's something the rest of us have to work to obtain.

Being able to express what we feel in words is essential as well. We must be able to convey verbally our deep appreciation for our children. Although I do not believe in cheapening affection by expressing it too often in merely sentimental terms, I do think that if we accustom ourselves to express our appreciation and love for our children regularly, it will make it possible for even deeper communication to occur when special moments arise. It will also help to prevent situations like the one Will Glennon describes in his book *Fathering*.

> My father came over to see me on a Saturday, very agitated. He'd been listening to a talk radio program about fathers and a number of callers had been complaining about how much it had hurt that their fathers never told them they loved them. I can remember at least three times my father told me he loved me, but

he couldn't remember and was worried that he had really blown it. There we were in the garage, me trying to finish some doll-house furniture I had promised my daughter and him trying to figure out how to say "I love you." It took him nearly an hour, and I think it was the hardest thing he ever did in his life.

It wasn't hard for this father to love his son. It just had become increasingly difficult for him to express that love out of a lack of practice.

## THOUGHTFULLY AWARE

Any undertaking that asks for our best will require heightened awareness. In our most serious endeavors we are attentive and thoughtful on so many levels. We know that we simply can't do a job well if we aren't sufficiently thoughtful. Fathering is no different. It requires that a mindful state of awareness influence our actions and our emotional responses.

This thoughtful awareness will require an alert and wakeful state of mind. The price we *pay* for a good relationship with our children is that we *pay attention*. We will not be able to achieve this if we are living in the past, preoccupied, our thoughts still dwelling on the events of the workday. Similarly, we cannot get ahead of ourselves and be concerned or worried about something that we need to do tomorrow. Instead, we must be like Ken Singleton coming to the plate, completely present in the moment. Truly great hitters like Shoeless Joe Jackson and Ted Williams knew that it was the absolute focus of their attention that made them so effective.

Because we lead busy lives, our children will come to us most often when we are in the middle of other work. Fathers who can give their complete attention to their children, at least long enough to see what is being asked, are truly special. Some of Abraham Lincoln's cabinet members complained that Lincoln would willingly drop everything to attend to his children when they interrupted his White House meetings.

Fathering will challenge us to be mentally alert despite the fact that we feel drained at the end of the day. After a late night, a long commute, or an exhausting day, we may feel beat, if not beaten. Little by little we have to rouse ourselves and attend. We have to develop the ability to become watchful before we respond so that we don't act or speak without thinking. Our thoughtful awareness needs to intercede between our children's actions and our immediate and sometimes regrettable response. The cool, reflective power of our thinking is the perfect antidote for the hot flash of anger that can plague fathers.

Most of all, we need a framework to help us understand our children and their behavior. We need an effective way of comprehending why our children act the way they do and how we can interact with them in a meaningful way. To understand our children, their development, and our role as parents, we need a conceptual framework, one that will enable us to see our children in a new way and better understand what they need from us.

# UNDERSTAND THE PACE OF THE GAME AND MANAGE ACCORDINGLY

◆

LIKE BASEBALL, CHILDHOOD HAS ITS EARLY, MIDDLE, AND LATE INNINGS. EACH PERIOD REQUIRES ITS OWN STRATEGY TO MEET ITS PARTICULAR NEEDS. HERE'S WHAT THEY ARE AND HOW TO HANDLE THEM.

Baseball's magic number is three. Three strikes and you're out, three outs in an inning, three outfield positions, the triple crown, the triple play, and three runners on base when they're loaded. Even the nine-inning game divides neatly into three segments: the early innings, middle innings, and late innings. Childhood also has its early, middle, and late innings, and each of these phases lasts about seven years.

In baseball, the boundaries between the three segments are clearly marked. When you reach the top of the fourth, the middle innings begin. In childhood, the boundary between each phase is not as precise. It is more like the change of seasons. We know that spring begins on March 21, but the weather does not always change noticeably on that day. And yet, as we approach that date, the sun is higher in the sky, the birds sing more robustly, and baseball stories begin to appear again on the front page of the sports section. Spring itself comes in waves. Several weeks past the equinox, there is no doubt it has arrived. That is how children

13

change from one phase to another—gradually, but convincingly. Depending on the child, spring can come a little early or a little late, but it will come.

Childhood's framework is also cast in threes. Children, notoriously active, emotional, and thoughtful, will meet us in the same three-dimensional way that we need to meet them as was outlined in chapter one. They will develop actively as toddlers, emotionally in the middle years, and thoughtfully as teenagers.

## THE ACTIVE CHILD

Anyone who has tried to keep up with toddlers for an entire day knows how central activity is to their experience of the world. In the first phase of child development, from birth until around the age of seven, children are overwhelmingly active; they learn by doing. Therefore, all of the activity that is done in their presence is of the greatest importance. Children's experience of the world is immediate and unmediated: What they see being done they actively imitate, and few actions escape their notice. Their need to be active is expressed through this overwhelming urge to imitate.

Imitation, of course, never leaves us completely; human beings imitate at all ages. Teenagers imitate their peers. I have seen graduate students imitate their professors' ideas, speech, and even gestures. We all have probably met adults who imitate the speech and habits of people that they admire. Yet at no time is the desire to imitate as pronounced and relentless as it is in early childhood. The imitative experience is far more pervasive than we usually imagine. It is the fundamental way that little children learn about the world they live in. Imitation has such force that through it a child can grasp all the intricacies of learning a language, with its complex vocabulary, intonation, inflection, and syntax.

This desire to imitate is so primary for children that they will imitate without reservation. It is as if young children are born with the conviction that the world is good and all that is done in their presence is worthy of emulation. Consequently, all of our actions are important.

When I was a child I would wait on the stoop each day for my father to come home from work. I would stand there looking up the street with two baseball gloves and a ball in my hand. The first words out of my mouth were always the same: "Can we have a catch?" My dad was a refrigeration engineer and a steamfitter, and often his days were physically demanding. I can never recall him saying that he was too tired to play. So we would stand out on the narrow sidewalk in front of our house on a fairly busy New York City street and throw a ball. I can still see him in my mind standing there as I tried my fancy pitches. He was anticipating my wildness and I never let him down. Invariably, one of my errant throws would evade him and roll into the street where a car or a bus would hit it and send it farther down the block, a decent walk from where we stood. It was then that my father would give me an exasperated look, a look that seemed to say both "I knew that you were going to do that" and "How many times have I told you...."

Many years later I was sitting at the kitchen table with my younger son, who was a lot like I was as a child. We were eating lunch and he was playing with his milk when suddenly the glass tipped over and the milk spilled all over the table. The first thing I thought was that I knew he was going to do that, and then, how many times I had told him not to play with his glass. Without saying a word it happened. I gave him *the look*. I couldn't see my face, but I knew that it was the very same look that my dad used to give me. It was mine now. Not because I wanted it, but just because so often what we see as children we become, like it or not.

Our actions affect our children throughout their entire life. What we do in the presence of our children in these early years could easily dispose them to similar actions later on. Our actions provide the foundation for our children's understanding of the world, and they learn by watching us. Our interactions with other people, with our spouses, and with the outside world condition our children to respond similarly. But like the foundation of a building, much of this essential work remains below the surface, unseen, and we are usually not aware of how deeply it influences what develops later.

When my father passed away a few years back, my mother asked me to speak at the funeral service. I decided to speak about all that my dad had taught me. As I looked out into the church, I could see all my parents' friends seated in the pews, and there was my dad's casket at the front of the center aisle. I was once told that when our parents die we experience our own mortality. This was indeed the case for me. As I began to speak, I looked up and saw my two sons and my daughter. I realized that one day my children would stand and speak about my life as I was about to speak about my dad's.

To begin, I recounted the simple things my father had taught me. I mentioned being taught how to drive a car and to use a handsaw (pull, don't push). I recounted how he taught me to swim and to throw a spiral with a football. I wanted to apologize to the priest seated behind me and mention all the expletives my father had unintentionally taught me. I knew that my father would have had a good laugh had I been less timid.

Eventually, I spoke about all that my father had taught me implicitly rather than explicitly, for this is an even bigger part of what we teach our children. Just by virtue of who he was and how he lived his life, my father had taught me how important it was to spend time with my family. Without ever so much as saying a word, he taught me not to gamble and not to drink more than an occasional beer. He also taught me that when you tell someone you are going to do something, you do it. He was always a man of his word, and I admired that.

As I spoke, I realized that my father was still teaching me. He was showing me in no uncertain terms that who we are influences who our children become in the most fundamental way. This is the primary opportunity and the burden of parenting. Our young children are completely unreserved in how they give themselves to this activity of imitation, and they have no way to filter out what is unworthy. This is the vulnerability of young children. They are so trusting and loving that they merge completely with their environment, for better or worse. We must understand the imitative nature of the young child and how it requires that adults provide worthy examples through their behavior.

Rudolf Steiner mentioned this responsibility in his book, *The Education of the Child*.

> Two "magic" words—*imitation* and *example*—indicate how children enter into relationship with their environment. The Greek philosopher Aristotle called human beings the most imitative of creatures. For no age in life is this truer than for the first stage of childhood. It includes not just what happens around children in the material sense, but everything that can be perceived by their senses, that can work on the inner powers of children from the surrounding physical space. It includes all moral or immoral actions, all wise or foolish actions that children see.

Many young people today sense that they bear the burdens of their parents' deeds. Children who have experienced alcoholism and drug dependency, abuse (physical, verbal, or sexual), even divorce, feel vulnerable to repeat the events that caused them so much pain. It is as if they are bound by the chains of the past, and only the most conscientious and directed effort will enable them to prevail. Unconsciously, they sense that the actions done in their presence at such an impressionable age have become part of them and they are now at risk.

Australian author Steve Biddulph takes this idea a step further and underscores the particular importance of a father's actions. "Most of us have discovered, uneasily, that we have gestures, mannerisms, or ways of doing things that are exactly those of our father. Deep down inside we stand on all kinds of foundations which we must get to know, allow for and understand." Because we see mounting evidence that the sins of the past are revisited on the present, we look for the root cause in genetics. However, a limited approach can obscure the truth. Children's behaviors are also learned, and they are learned at a time when they are most impressionable.

It is clear that our actions influence our young children. Fathers who want to have a more significant role in raising their children will look for meaningful ways to be active at home and then strive to be worthy of their children's imitation. For the first seven years of childhood, this is parents' most important task, for the effects of these actions will be evident throughout childhood and even in our children's adult lives.

## THE EMOTIONAL CHILD

As children grow toward grade school, many changes occur. Around the age of six or seven, their arms, legs, and features lengthen; they lose their baby teeth and their baby fat. At this time changes go on in the inner life of the child as well. Their play becomes more imaginative, and their feelings begin to play a more prominent role in their experience of the world. For children in the middle innings of childhood, *feelings* are the substance that fills their lives with that magical, childlike quality; they are the sustenance on which children thrive.

Think of the richness of the feelings of your own childhood: the protective feeling of security and safety when you were tucked into a warm bed with clean sheets on a cold night, the feeling of promise that was conveyed by the morning sun and a fragrant breeze on a Saturday morning in May, or the deeply private feeling of a cold and cloudy afternoon in November when the days were short and you were heading home for dinner. This second stage of childhood is filled with likes and dislikes, when both joy and sorrow can cause a child's cup to run over.

Fathers find it hard to recapture these feelings. In the rush of our busy lives it is nearly impossible to recall the sheer joy of just being out at night or the unbearable pleasure of sleeping at a friend's house for the first time. It is also hard to fathom the depths of a child's sorrow, the disappointment when special plans change, or the heartbreak when a pet dies. If we are to continue to play a meaningful role in our children's lives when they enter this second phase of childhood, we will have to find a way to meet our children on an emotional level.

It makes sense that fathers find it challenging to relate to their children in this way. Fifty years ago, emotional responsiveness was not part of a father's job description. Consequently, many men did not experience their own fathers relating in an emotional way. It is also hard for fathers to live fully in their feelings without assuming an aspect of vulnerability that is not valued in either the workplace or society.

Feelings, both our children's and ours, are obscure. They

reside in a region of our consciousness that is hard to engage directly and often harder to understand. To enhance our work as fathers we should take a closer look at an aspect of our children's lives that may at first seem unrelated, but that will have a direct impact on our emotional relationship with our children: the passage of time. Each year, each season, each week, each day, can help us form an emotional connection with our child.

Given the busyness of our lives, we often simply lack time to feel things deeply, and yet time is something our children can have in abundance. Time is something that baseball also has in abundance—an echo of another era when lives were simpler and there was even enough time to play a doubleheader. Baseball's timelessness gave it its unique character. It allowed space for rituals like infield practice between innings and warm-up pitches. (Can you picture a quarterback making a few warm-up tosses to his wide receivers on the field when the starting quarterback has been pulled or unlimited tosses if the starting quarterback has been injured?)

Like childhood, baseball has extensive stretches of routine, uneventful play and then moments of dramatic excitement; the true fan loves both equally. It is just this element of time that makes it possible for indelible impressions to be formed and for the game to work its way into our hearts. If fathers can recall their own childhood experience of time, they will be better able to relate to their children on an emotional level.

One way in which children entering the middle innings of their childhood come to terms with time is by separating it into categories. They begin to notice the difference between weekdays and weekends, between workdays and holidays, and between the school year and vacation. Over time they attach positive and negative feelings to these distinctions. Eventually, the child's world gets divided into two categories—the common everyday and the uncommonly special. This is a crucial distinction for fathers, for we need to play a role in each category. We need to enliven and lighten the common and everyday so that it doesn't become heavy, tedious, and monotonous. We also need to make memorable those times that are uncommonly special. But when fathers, like the great players, are able to make the everyday and routine into something uncommonly special, we work wonders.

Dealing with the everyday routines—dinner, homework, chores, music lessons, bedtime—will present its own set of challenges for the father. Our interactions will add either buoyancy or heaviness to the family mood, depending on our mood. If we are able to enter into each activity with newness, appreciation, and lightheartedness, our arrival at home will be anticipated each day. Our emotional climate has the power to alter the family's emotional weather conditions dramatically. In the movie *Life Is Beautiful*, Roberto Benigni plays a character who does just this. His mood is so jubilant that it keeps his child's spirits soaring in the midst of the everyday and in the face of the worst possible situation.

As every parent knows, the everyday routine always has its pitfalls. This means that we will need to find appropriate ways to express ourselves when we are disappointed and upset. During such moments, well-timed and well-expressed words are like safety valves that help us gently let off steam and reduce the pressure. In all our interactions we need to be aware of the temperature of our words. The warmth of our words should draw our children toward us. We should guard ourselves against the icy cold of sarcasm or criticism and the hot flash of anger. Here again, we will be reminded that fatherhood calls for our very best, our better self.

"When a man lives with God, his voice shall be as sweet as the murmur of the brook and the rustle of the corn." I have always loved this statement of Ralph Waldo Emerson. It's not that I can do this in my life, but if the day ever arrives when I can speak to my daughter during our common and everyday routines and my voice is this sweet, I will rejoice.

The special events in our children's lives give us the opportunity to experience the passage of time in a deeply satisfying way. This time apart from the everyday routine enables us to relax and unwind.

Nearly every Thanksgiving our family travels to New York City. Because this is the most heavily traveled weekend and because we have experienced some unbelievable traffic jams, we have become accustomed to leaving our house at about 5:30 on Thursday morning. This helps us avoid the holiday traffic and puts us in New York City at about 10:00 a.m. Instead of heading directly to my mother's for our family gathering, we take some time and go to the Macy's Thanksgiving Day Parade. We avoid the crowds on the street, park our car near Fifth Avenue, and head for the Empire State Building. There, from the observation deck, we look down on the parade. We can't hear the music. We can barely see the marching bands. But we have the most unusual view of the balloons as they make their way downtown. It is a memorably surreal sight to see Woody Woodpecker or Betty Boop rising above the buildings and listing over Herald Square as the parade passes the reviewing stand, an experience that leaves us feeling that work and school responsibilities have receded and the uncommonly special has arrived.

I have always felt that part of my job description as a father was to help make these special events in my children's lives occur in a predictably rhythmic fashion. Halloween, Thanksgiving, Chanukah, Christmas, birthdays, vacations are all awaited on the calendar of the year's events. Effective fathers will involve themselves in these events by creating rituals that are connected to each special occasion. When special occurrences happen in a predictable way, they become traditions that touch a child's heart. When they evoke good feelings, feelings fostered by smiles and laughs, made firm by songs and friends and conversations, they will be a greater gift to our children than any present we could buy for them. Sometimes, however, the truly special moment takes everyone, including us, by surprise.

For a number of years our family made it a tradition to go to opening day. In 1981 that opportunity presented itself twice. When the prolonged midsummer baseball strike ended, a second season began in August. Tired of following the Charleston Charlies and the Toledo Mud Hens (which had been our only local choices during the strike), we decided to give major league baseball another chance.

The Baltimore Orioles opened against the Kansas City Royals, and we were in the stands. Late in the game Orioles' manager Earl Weaver sent in a pinch runner, a highly touted prospect who scored the winning run: Cal Ripken. My sons and I have always been pleased that we saw Ripken's first big-league game. There was no way I could have planned a memorable event like that. My sons still talk about the game sometimes; it makes us all feel a bit older that we can recall a time when Cal was valued for his speed.

## THE THOUGHTFUL CHILD

The late innings of childhood may find us looking to the bullpen for relief and muttering to ourselves, " Where's the closer?" It is during this third phase that our children, now teenagers, will ask more of us than ever before—and this makes sense. The end of the late innings will bring the culmination of our work as parents, a time when we hope that our children's capacity for independent thought and sound judgment has been fully developed. During these late innings, new demands will be placed on us because we will need to engage our daughters and sons vigorously in a new, dynamic way: through their thinking.

This new capacity for critical thinking, however, will also manifest in perplexing ways. As the capacity for critical thinking grows, young people flex their new mental muscles and are willing and eager to argue. It is parents' responsibility to help their children develop this thinking capacity, and we should do this by engaging them in lively, but friendly discussions. This new phase in child development, however, may take getting used to. Arguing is a form of wrestling for young people. It is a way to assess their new strength, and they will often throw their weight around. Fathers needn't panic at the surprising nature of some of their children's opinions. At this age, children try on new thoughts and opinions the way they try on new clothes to see how they fit and feel. They will test out opinions that they have heard at school or from friends in an effort to better understand them. And it is not uncommon for young people to express an opinion that is diametrically opposed to what they believe. I am of the mind that teenagers should be free to think what they like. However, that doesn't mean that they should *do* what they like.

First and foremost, fathers should show respect for their children's thinking. There is little at this age that is as discouraging as having your opinions dismissed with a perfunctory "Well, when you're older you will think differently," or having your point of view lumped into a single category and discarded with "You kids all think alike." A teenager's opinions on all sorts of subjects should be solicited regularly and listened to with interest. As a young person, I would have been genuinely surprised and duly impressed if my father had ever asked me what I thought about the war in Vietnam, and I am sure all of my strong opinions would have relaxed noticeably in the face of that openness.

The fourteen- and fifteen-year-olds that I have taught have always had an ample supply of opinions. And they were inclined to express these opinions in provocative ways, primarily for effect. However, whenever I turned to those same young people directly and solicited their opinion, a strange thing happened. They immediately expressed themselves in a more moderate and thoughtful manner. Fathers should always ask their children for their opinions on matters. You're going to hear them anyway, so you might as well initiate the conversation.

Teenagers are beginning a quest for truth. Regardless of how convoluted this search may appear at times, it is a noble undertaking. Teenagers would love to have their fathers along on this journey, if they are willing to search for the truth without assuming that they already know what it is. Fathers who can relinquish the role of instructor and become students again, who can see that "freshman year" is a worthy state of mind, will find their teenagers turning to them for company on their search for truth. This search for truth means considering issues from many points of view, and this thought process should be seen as calisthenics helping to strengthen our children's capacity to think.

If we take seriously our own search for truth, we will be forced to admit that there are many things that we simply do not know. We are much better suited to be learners than teachers. Still, there are stands that we as fathers will have to take and positions that we will have to defend regarding curfews, substance abuse, and teenage sex if we are to accept our responsibility as fathers and not try to be only buddies to our teenagers.

By standing firmly for what we believe, we give our young people something to push against, and this too is a gift. This resistance helps not only define us, it defines them by helping them to begin to know where they stand. We want to give our children good values, and we want to give them a sense of who they are. The more we are able to clarify our beliefs through conversation and discussion, the more our children will be able to develop theirs by resisting ours. In the long run we don't want our kids to grow up to think like us; rather we want them, in the truest sense, to think for themselves, and this, of course, will take time and a great deal of effort.

Forming and expressing beliefs is not the only area where our teenagers will need our help. The growing physical strength found in a teenager's rapidly developing body needs outlets for purposeful activity. Although they can spend vast amounts of time doing nothing, teenagers are happier and healthier when they are active. At this stage it is no longer as necessary that we participate in the activities with our children so much as that we support and encourage their participation. Teenagers like to test limits, and this is true of physical activity as well.

A number of years ago the state of California offered a work program for young people similar to the Civilian Conservation Corps, the federally funded program during the Depression. The California program advertised itself as offering hard work, low pay, and long hours. It had a waiting list.

Teenagers will also begin to demonstrate keen interest in diverse activities. Music, mountain bikes, computers, horses, skateboards, and political causes will captivate their attention and dominate their conversations. Fathers need to show an interest in the activities that interest our children, and when our children ask us to look and listen, we need to make time.

Teenagers should also have a skill that they can do as well as an adult. It is especially important for fathers to sense where and when our teenage children's interests should be encouraged and sustained. These interests can lead to practical abilities and life-long talents. I have heard it said that if we can help our children acquire the ability to do something as well as an adult, we have given them a gift for life. This ability could be in any field— emergency rescue, bicycle and automobile repair, bread baking, carpentry, instrumental music, animal husbandry—it doesn't really matter, as long as young people feel that there is something real at which they are proficient. This will give them a sense of self-worth as well as a talent that they will enjoy and continue to develop in the years to come.

A number of years ago I went to observe a unique educational program in a local high school, in which a number of students were being taught how to build houses. One of the houses was complete and up for sale, so I went to the open house. I was struck by the fine work that the students had done and sought out one of the teachers. I asked him how the students felt about their accomplishment. He said that the students were often reticent to express their satisfaction. Sometimes, he said, they would bring their parents to see the houses. They would walk through the rooms with their hands in their pockets, looking at the floor, while their parents looked around. Eventually a father or mother would ask, "What part did you work on?" The students, I was told, would hem and haw and then modestly admit that they had wired the entire kitchen and hung all the kitchen cabinets, or built the main staircase. They would say this in an understated way as if it were no big deal. But on another level, the teacher said, you could sense the fullness of their satisfaction and pleasure.

Someday these young people will come to see the full value

of what they have acquired. This skill will also give them the opportunity to relate to adults as equals, and this is something for which they long. To be depended on by adults is a gratifying and new experience for a teenager, one that leads to an experience of their own growing independence. Working side by side with adults as an equal is an important experience for young people, one that they will value.

I recently encountered a father at a parenting conference in Canada who was troubled because he had lost the ability to interact with his teenage son in a positive and fulfilling way. He and his son were unable to communicate, and there was no place where their lives seemed to intersect. I asked the father to tell me the last time that he had a meaningful encounter with his son. He thought for a moment and then recalled a day when his son helped him and a number of other men to repave the driveway. He described how happy his son was working alongside these other men. This experience illustrates the value of being accepted as an equal. Developing a working knowledge in a particular skill area will produce a similarly gratifying experience, a sense of coming of age.

In addition to rigorous activity, our children will continue to need our emotional support and affirmation. Physically they are nearly adults, but on an emotional level they are still uncertain. Teenagers turn to us for this support, often at unusual times. Parents who wait up for their seventeen- and eighteen-year-olds find that the time they get to talk most is around midnight. Around midnight, some teenagers will open up and confide in ways that they never would during the normal hours of the day. It is true that the times that our children need us diminish markedly as they grow older, but in this last stage of childhood, being deprived of sleep can again be a common experience for parents.

Different children need varying amounts of maintenance. Our second son is a fine young man, but he asked more of us than either his brother or sister. This was always clear when he returned home from college for visits. He would regularly leave school for fall break, holidays, or at the end of the semester in the late afternoon and begin the seven-hour ride home from Ohio with friends. Toward the end of his college days it became a ritual that he would get dropped off at home at about 1:00 a.m. He'd put his bags in his room and immediately come into our bedroom and sit down on the bed. Here's this 200-pound college athlete, a left-handed power hitter who played in the NCAA College World Series, sitting on the bed and talking about his exams, his plans for the break, and the status of his relationship with his girlfriend as if this were a conversation taking place over breakfast. Although such conversations could be a little exhausting, a parent would never want to miss that opportunity.

To help our children to grow toward independence, we must understand their developmental journey and meet each of their three main developmental needs. All three of these aspects are present in each phase but with a different emphasis for our involvement: early innings, active; middle innings, emotional; and late innings, thoughtful. Perhaps, as we stop to pick up the three small stones at the doorstep before we enter the house, we will recall that each stone can also represent one of the three ways that our children will need to be engaged in order for us to have a complete game.

## TO BE AN ALL-STAR, MAKE THE HIGHLIGHT FILM (AND AVOID THE BLOOPER REEL)

◆

LIKE A BASEBALL SEASON, FATHERING WILL GIVE RISE TO A COLLECTION OF MEMORIES. CRUCIAL SAVES AND LATE-INNING TRIUMPHS WILL LEAVE A STRONG IMPRESSION —BUT SO WILL EMBARRASSING ERRORS AND DISAPPOINTING STRIKEOUTS. HERE'S HOW TO FOSTER POSITIVE MEMORIES WHILE AVOIDING THE NEGATIVE ONES.

*You must know that there is nothing higher and stronger and more wholesome and good for life in the future than some good memory, especially a memory of childhood, of home. People talk to you a good deal about your education, but some good sacred memory, preserved from your childhood, is perhaps the best education. If a man carries many such memories with him into life, he is safe to the end of his days. And if one has only one good memory left in one's heart, even that may sometimes be the means of saving him.*

—FYODOR DOSTOYEVSKY, *The Brothers Karamazov*

I was sure that it was going to be a memorable event. The Baltimore Orioles were playing an exhibition game against the Philadelphia Phillies in Washington, D.C. (our hometown), in April, and this would be a unique opportunity to see a game in town. I ordered tickets early and got us all seats in the first row in left field. Having read that it was only 275 feet down the line in RFK Stadium, I imagined us chasing batting practice home runs and having a vivid and unencumbered experience of the game.

When that April day finally arrived, the weather was cold and wet, but the game was on. Batting practice, of course, was cancelled, the seats weren't great, and by game time it was snowing. We shivered through five innings of uninspired baseball and when the game was official and no refunds were necessary, it was called.

A second experience shows a remarkable contrast. When my oldest son was six, we shared our first baseball season together. The year was 1979 and the Orioles were having a magical start to their season. This was also the time of the oil embargo, rising gas prices, and gas lines. I arranged to ride to work with others that week to save my gas, knowing that on Sunday we would make the long drive up to Memorial Stadium in Baltimore to watch the Orioles play an afternoon game against Texas.

It turned out to be a beautiful Sunday in June. The school year had just ended, and this shed an aura of ease over the day's affairs. We sat in reserved seats behind third base, but as the game progressed we moved down into the empty box seats in front of us and enjoyed the game in the sun. Around the fourth or fifth inning the opposing team had runners on first and second and no outs. Buddy Bell came to bat and ripped a line drive down the third base line. As we watched, the Orioles' third baseman grabbed that line drive and began a triple play. It happened suddenly and unexpectedly on this peaceful Sunday afternoon, but we saw it so clearly. It left an indelible impression on my son as well. As a grown man, he still remembers the blue of those old Texas uniforms, that the line drive was hit to Doug DeCinces, and that the triple play went "around the horn."

You can't always plan for a truly memorable event. It obviously needs the convergence of special circumstances. But a truly memorable event does have certain prerequisites. It requires that our three-dimensional involvement—our active, emotional, and thoughtful awareness—coincide with that same level of involvement from our children. This means that we will need to do something special together, and that we must both take part in an open-hearted and joyful way. In addition, a truly memorable event will usually require thoughtful planning and an element of surprise and newness, something to help focus our attention.

One wonderful example of this is found in Doris Kearns Goodwin's memoir, *Wait Till Next Year*. In this exceptional book, the author relates a remarkable and yet simple ritual that she observed with her father:

> When I was six, my father gave me a bright-red scorebook that opened my heart to the game of baseball. After dinner on long summer nights, he would sit beside me in our small, enclosed porch to hear my account of that day's Brooklyn Dodger game. Night after night he taught me the odd collection of symbols, numbers, and letters that enable a baseball lover to record every action of the game. Our score sheets had blank boxes in which we could draw our own slanted lines in the form of a diamond as we followed players around the bases. Wherever the baserunner's progress stopped, the line stopped. He instructed me to fill in the unused boxes at the end of each inning with an elaborate checkerboard design which made it absolutely clear who had been the last to bat and who would lead off the next inning. By the time I had mastered the art of scorekeeping, a lasting bond had been forged among my father, baseball, and me.

All during a summer of baseball, this young girl would listen to the

Dodgers' games in the afternoon and keep score. When her father came home after work, they would sit together and she would recount the game batter by batter, using her scorebook and keeping her father in suspense. On those days when her father came home knowing the outcome of the day's game, he would never let on.

## LETTING OUR OWN CHILDHOOD MEMORIES GUIDE US

I met recently with a group of fathers near Charlottesville, Virginia, and in the course of that meeting I asked a simple question: What do you remember most strongly from your relationship with your father? The responses were wide ranging.

There was one father who grew up on a small village farm in Europe and spent every day in the fields with his father. His eyes grew bright as he described working by his father's side and the horse-drawn cart where he took his naps. Other men spoke of solitary fathers who sought nightly refuge at a workbench in the basement where they isolated themselves from their children and their wives. And others had grown up without fathers. When these men spoke, there was a poignant sense of the great emptiness caused by a father's absence.

These responses, however, were not unusual. Actually, they were very similar to the responses I had heard in other cities. I am always moved when I listen to such recollections, because these memories of childhood are still permeated with childlike feelings. You can hear the feelings when they catch on the spoken words; you can see the feelings in the eyes of these grown men, revealing the tender part in each of us where our fathers have left their mark. These recollections remind us of how deeply our fathers have affected us.

Our childhood memories are tremendously important, for they bear within them the secret to creating memorable experiences with our own children. When the men that I have worked with in fathering workshops and seminars recalled their own memories, common elements emerged: age-appropriate activities, good moods for both parents and children, and new, surprising, and instructive situations. But there is one other important element that is often part of good childhood memories, and that is the tradition of doing something special again and again.

## BUILDING A FAMILY TRADITION
## OF MEMORABLE EVENTS

Repeated activities become family traditions, and they can actually be the simplest routines. One story that I heard was told by a man who spent little time with his own father. In the summertime, he would spend his vacation with relatives in the country. Each evening he would go for a ride in his uncle's pickup truck, and they would drive into town together to see the 8:15 train roll by. This man could still remember the songs his uncle sang as they drove along the country road. The carefree feeling on those summer evenings, the excitement stirred by the presence of that powerful train, and the growing bond between this boy and his uncle, made firm through a simple song, helped etch this memory deep into the child's soul so that years later he would value it as one of his most precious recollections.

Simple impressions can yield lasting memories, like the smell of a leather baseball glove held close to our face. Scents are deeply connected to our memories. Perhaps that is why food plays a prominent role in the childhood memories that I have heard fathers retell. Just think back. Was there a diner where your father took you regularly for breakfast? Can't you still remember what you ordered? Was there a bakery where he stopped each week? If there was, do you remember how delightful it was to see the white bakery box tied with string and to open it, to look inside and just smell that delicious aroma?

It is especially on weekends that fathers can create traditions connected with food. If we are up first and ready to go, we can play our trump card. Fathers and food can be a successful combination, especially when it comes to breakfast. What will the ritual be? Will we go out and buy bagels and lox, orange juice, or donuts? Will we make eggs, French toast, or pancakes? Regardless of the menu, or whether it's breakfast, lunch, or supper, fathers should be part of the memories connected with food.

I have a special fondness for dishes that look elaborate but are really easy to make. One summer while we were on vacation at the beach with friends, I watched with admiration as a single mom prepared a delicious breakfast for a half dozen teenagers in a matter of minutes. I made sure that I got the recipe. Here it is in a scaled-down version.

## FRENCH TOAST

3 eggs
½ cup of milk
½ teaspoon of vanilla
½ teaspoon of cinnamon
6 to 8 slices of bread

Mix these ingredients together in a pie plate or deep dish and then soak each slice of bread in the mixture for about ten seconds on each side. Then place a pat of butter in a frying pan and cook the

French toast over a low flame until brown on both sides. Top with maple syrup, jam, or yogurt and fresh fruit. This is delicious, yet simple and quick; the recipe tastes like it takes a lot longer to make.

Food and fathers is a winning combination, and it is certainly the matchup we want. Everything is in our favor. We can be a little expedient and nobody minds. We can deviate from normal nutritional standards on occasion, and it's all right. When a pitcher covers home there are different expectations than when the catcher is there. The important thing is that we're getting the job done, and creating lasting memories in the process.

## MAKING MEMORIES IN NATURE

Camping trips, also rich with the smell of food cooked on an open fire, provide many fathers and their children with memorable experiences. The rhythmic occurrence of an annual camping trip, the unusualness of the surroundings and the routines, the sense of adventure, the sights, and the sounds make an indelible impression on our children.

Almost every year for the past sixteen years, our family has camped in a national park in Maine. As our long drive north would near its end, the questions would begin to surface, showing that the memories were still alive. Can we go to the ranger show tonight? Can we hike Cadillac Mountain tomorrow? Can we swim at Sand Beach? Do you think we'll be able to hike the Precipice Trail this year?

The Precipice Trail is the most challenging climb in Acadia National Park. It has a 1,000-foot ascent up the steep face of Mount Champlain. There are numerous places where the climb is precipitous, and climbers have to use metal rungs and ladders to make their way up the steep rock face. We first took our sons on this hike when they were eight and twelve years old, and images of that day are still fresh in our minds. In recent years, however, the trail has been closed in the summer to protect the peregrine falcons that nest in the cliffs. For the past couple of summers our daughter has yearned to do this hike as a rite of passage and as a point of honor. Having heard the stories, she did not want to be outdone by her brothers. This September she got her wish. We hiked the trail on a brilliant autumn day and got to see the young peregrine falcons flying nearby; both she and the falcons were spreading their wings. I imagine that there will come a time when our children will take their children on this hike.

The sense of newness and adventure is essential, especially as our children get older. Activities that take place outdoors can elicit a good mixture of excitement and awe. Those unusual moments—when a buck bolts from the woods onto the trail in front of us, when an eagle rises from a treetop just above us, or when an owl hoots in the dead of night—will sear themselves into our children's memories, treasures that cannot be purchased. The following statement by Barry Angell bears this out completely.

Yesterday, my eleven-year-old son and I were hiking in a remote wood. He was leading. He spotted a four-foot rattlesnake in the trail about six feet in front of us. We watched it for quite some time before going around it. When we were on the way home, he commented that this was the best day of his life. He was justifiably proud of the fact that he had been paying attention and thus had averted an accident, and that he had been able to observe this powerful, beautiful, and sinister snake.

## MAKING THOUGHTFUL MEMORIES

By now it should be evident that there is a bias in my approach to fathering; I like to be active. But what about the father whose activity is inward? There are, of course, other memorable ways to interact with our children, and these will have more to do with emotional and thoughtful interactions. I learned this firsthand from a father who took his son and a group of friends to the ocean each summer. This father and his wife rented a large beach house and invited a half dozen of their son's friends and their families as well. The teenage boys rode their bikes, swam in the ocean, ate almost continuously, and played marathon games of wiffle-ball on the beach while this father watched and read. He loved books and shared them with the kids. He bought them books, recommended books, took them to the library, and continually engaged them in conversation about what they read. He dubbed these fellows "the boys of summer" and helped them develop in so many ways. And though he never threw a pitch or rode a wave, he provided them with an opportunity for the most incredible memories.

## MAKING MEMORIES THAT
## DON'T MAKE $ENSE

Sometimes creating memorable experiences won't make sense financially. When given a choice between remodeling the bathroom, buying new carpet, or going on a family vacation, from a memory standpoint, we would do well to choose the vacation.

A few summers ago I was invited to work with teachers at a school in Calgary, Alberta. Our family had always talked about a cross-country trip and this seemed to be a good opportunity, perhaps the last opportunity. At the time our sons were twenty and twenty-four and it was becoming harder and harder to find extended periods of time for us all to be together. In planning this trip it became clear that we could take two weeks to drive out west, camping along the way, but our sons would have to fly back from Calgary to return for work and for school. Calgary is not an air travel hub of Canada, and, as it turned out, two one-way tickets home would cost more than $1,000, a most uneconomical expense. We did it anyway. In fact, it may have been the best thousand dollars we ever spent. Our trip to the Badlands, the Black Hills, Yellowstone, and Banff was worth every penny. And what's more, it really was our last opportunity to travel like that together. From an economic standpoint this trip was a complete failure. From our family's memory standpoint, this trip made the highlight film.

## TRYING TO AVOID MAKING BAD MEMORIES

I don't like to end a chapter on a sour note, but there are memories that we need to be sure to avoid making. Someone once asked me how I had changed as a teacher over twenty-five years. The best way that I could express myself was to use an analogy from baseball. When I first started out in the classroom I was like a young pitcher who throws hard but lacks finesse. After years of experience, I had finally learned how to pitch, how to merge thoughtfulness with activity, and most important, how to stay out of *the big inning*. When Earl Weaver managed the Orioles he would regularly point out that in most games the team that lost gave up more runs in one inning than it was able to score in the whole game. He understood the potential for ruin that is in the big inning when calamitous events completely overshadow all our other efforts. As fathers we have to learn to stay out of disastrous innings, when our errors and our lack of control make such a mess. When angry words and angry actions inflame a difficult situation, we need to step off the mound and call time before we say or do things unintentionally that move us toward the flash point. Explosive events will be remembered for years and will overshadow many of the good things that we do for our children.

Because what we experience with strong feelings gives rise to strong memories, we need to guard against dramatic and traumatic events in emotionally charged situations. Fathers need to be ever watchful at emotional times such as holidays, birthdays, and vacations, when a child's heart opens in anticipation, to avoid arguments and fights that can leave an indelible mark on children. We also need to look at our own painful memories, as well as the painful memories of other fathers, and allow these memories to guide us.

When we consider our unpleasant memories, the same three-dimensional framework is clearly evident. Many men still recall the sting of having their serious, but youthful, thoughts dismissed as childish and immature rather than elicited and explored through interested conversation. Other men remember the great sense of longing they had for heartfelt contact with a father who was emotionally unresponsive or their fear of the father who responded with unpredictable emotions and rage. And on the most fundamental level, there are those who simply remember looking up at a school event and seeing that their father was just not present. Having seen this pattern repeatedly in the memories that I have heard fathers share, I am convinced that the way to be remembered as a good father is to consciously balance our thoughtful, emotional, and active involvement with our children.

## Making Peace with Some Memories
## from Childhood

Not all that we remember from our own childhood is positive. There may be memories of our own fathers that sadden or anger us. When these memories surface, they should remind us that we still have to develop a deeper understanding of our own fathers. Steve Biddulph devotes a chapter to this topic in his book, *Manhood*, and has good advice to give. If there are hard feelings, a conversation is in order, one that has to take place while our fathers are still alive. Biddulph urges us to make the time to have a long, private conversation with our fathers before it is too late and pose the question, "What was it like for you?"

As a teenager I longed to have serious conversations with my father and to speak with him about what mattered to me. These conversations never happened and I felt shortchanged until I understood what adolescence had been like for him. When he was a boy of eleven, his father, who was only thirty-nine years old, was dying of black lung disease. This was during the Depression, and there was no disability or medical insurance, so his father had to keep working. They would walk together to the coal mines in the morning and his father would have to stop every few steps to catch his breath, just like an old man. Within a year his father was dead. When I heard this story, I understood how it had affected my father and how it affected me. My father was not skilled at having conversations with his teenage sons because he had never experienced them himself and had no memories to guide him. Coming to this realization helped me to have much more sympathy for my dad as well as to understand why it was harder for him to interact with me as I grew older.

## GOOD HABITS LAST
## ALL SEASON LONG, SO ESTABLISH
## THEM EARLY AND PRACTICE
## THEM OFTEN

◆

ESTABLISHING GOOD HABITS FROM THE
OUTSET CAN MAKE ALL THE DIFFERENCE.
YET IT WILL TAKE A PROLONGED AND
DETERMINED EFFORT TO SUSTAIN THE
PROPER DISCIPLINE THROUGHOUT THE
ENTIRE SEASON OF CHILDHOOD. DIFFI-
CULT? MAYBE. BUT NOT IMPOSSIBLE.

The all-star break is the baseball season's midpoint. This event
divides the regular season into two halves with approximately the
same number of regular season games, but these two halves are by
no means equal. Spring training and the first eighty-one games of
the season are filled with preparation and promise. This promise is
present in the inflated early-season batting averages when even
journeymen can resemble Ty Cobb and Rogers Hornsby. A pitcher's
spring days can be filled with promise as well, as 5–0 records in
May hint of possible thirty-win seasons. By July, however, these
marks and others can be called into question.

The second half of the season is generally more real, less
forgiving, but in the end, if all goes well, ultimately more reward-
ing. The dog days will test a team's mettle. There will be setbacks
and losing streaks. Good teams are able to keep perspective when
things go bad, unlike the '64 Phillies and the '78 Red Sox, or

more recently the '98 Mets. Pressure builds in September, and in the span of a single week a season can appear lost and then suddenly found. Is the long season of childhood so different?

Childhood's midpoint occurs somewhere around the age of ten. From that time on fathering can also become more real and less forgiving. This is caused by a subtle, distinct, yet necessary change that takes place in the inner life of our children. This change leads to independence and a sense of individuality, but it can also feel like the closing of a door.

It is hard to miss the difference between the warmth and spontaneous closeness of young children, eager to sit on a parent's lap, and the cool, sometimes awkward reserve of teenagers who isolate themselves in their bedroom or in the basement. This change is all about distance and separation, and in this regard the age of ten is pivotal. What will matter greatly at this point is what was worked on in the "spring training" of childhood and how well those habits were established in the first half of the season.

During the second half of the season, our fathering will be called into question. Losing streaks are also inevitable for fathers, and when they come, morale can suffer. Masked defiance, hints of mutiny, untimely leaks of information, and outright dissension can all occur at the dining room table as well as in the clubhouse, and how we respond will make all the difference. Fathers need to be prepared for the demands of both parts of the long season of childhood.

## PREVENTING DISCIPLINARY SITUATIONS

Both halves of the season of childhood require discipline. The way we establish our discipline during the early part of the season will influence the way we handle the problems that will inevitably arise later. The word *discipline* has within it the word *disciple*. We are called on to lead the way so our children can follow. If we are able to establish proper behavior from the outset rather than achieving it through corrective measures, our children will be happier and so will we. When we do this well, it may appear as if we are doing almost nothing.

Back in the days of Earl Weaver, the Orioles prided themselves on teaching their young players the fundamentals of the game. You could see it in the small details, in the rotation on bunt coverage and with cut-off throws, in the quick pace of their pitchers, even in the way that those pitchers covered first base. This was the "Oriole Way." It was a discipline established from the outset through the right kind of instruction.

This is what fathers need, first and foremost, from the start: preventive discipline. In considering how preventive discipline can be established and maintained over the three stages of childhood, bedtime will serve as an example, because bedtime can easily be an issue throughout all our years of fathering.

Bedtime entails more than simply placing our children under the covers. On the front end it involves washing up, brushing teeth, and putting on pajamas. After a child is in bed it may involve a story, a prayer, a song, and a very important period of time from the moment when the lights go out until our child is actually asleep.

The fact is that when bedtime is a pleasant event, everyone is happier. So it is worth the effort to establish this routine in the right way. Knowing that the young child is imitative and especially attuned to our activity, it makes sense that we will need to be an active participant in this process. The best way to do this is to begin, once our child is old enough, to accompany him to the bathroom to wash up and to brush his teeth. It will be up to us to model for our young child everything that we want him to do. We will be thoughtfully aware of how we squeeze the toothpaste tube and that we replace the cap. We will adjust the flow and temperature of the water with same care with which we adjust the throttle on an engine. All that we do should have a sense of importance.

The same is true for changing clothes. We should walk our child through the sequence of events, showing him that each removed article of clothing has its proper place. The child takes this all in as our actions give order to the world. This is the spring training of childhood. We are working on fundamentals: "This is the way we do things in our home." We establish a ritual and a routine, and for this routine to be really effective, we will need to do things the same way each day.

As parents, we have time on our side. There is no rush. If we act in this way, day in and day out, for a year or two, the routine will be in place. This will demand a great deal from us. It is always easier to do something for your child as opposed to helping him to do it himself. The discipline that is required of us is significant but is certainly worth it, and in the end we will get our reward. Our children will end up responsible and independent. Around the age of six or seven our children will begin to want to brush their teeth and change their clothes on their own. This doesn't mean that we are suddenly off the hook; we still need to be present and active, only in a more subtle way.

Now as our children head off to the bathroom, we watch and listen, but we don't necessarily follow. We watch to see that they actually go into the bathroom, for a child's propensity for distraction is unequaled. We listen for running water so that we can be sure they are moving through the routine in a timely fashion. We should even discreetly check and see that the bathroom and the bedroom are in good shape: no water on the floor, the towel back on the rack, both shoes in the closet, dirty clothes in the laundry. We are still present in the process, but our children have assumed more responsibility. We have pulled back. This is a perfect example of how we work as fathers to help our children.

The actual getting into bed, however, will need more than just our active participation. This is an important transition in the day for a child, and we need to develop a feeling for how to make this special. This time of the day will require an artistic touch. Gentle lighting will assist the gradual movement from day to night and ease the way to sleep. A story and a song will usher in a quiet mood, and a prayer will bring closure to the day. It is remarkable how a ritual that moves a child gradually and meaningfully from wakefulness to sleep can relieve fear and uncertainty. Twenty minutes of quality bedtime can eliminate an hour of "I'm thirsty," " I can't sleep," and "I'm scared." Let's see this time as an investment on many levels; by working to establish this routine at an early age we will ensure painless bedtimes for years to come.

And yet, we should not lose sight of the fact that rough stretches in the schedule await us. Even if we are effective fathers actively helping our families to establish meaningful rituals for bedtime, there will still be difficulties. It is important to know that these difficulties will arise just because our children are normal and in spite of the fact that we are doing a good job. If we can anticipate these rough spots we will not be surprised and, consequently, we will be better able to act in an even-tempered way.

So what can we expect? I believe that most children will test us at some point by either ignoring, resisting, or modifying the ritual. Somewhere around the age of nine or ten you may ask your child, "Did you brush your teeth and wash up?" and she will reply, "Yes." But you won't be sure. Or you might walk by the bathroom and hear the water running in the sink. However, when you look in the bathroom, you may see your daughter reading a Nancy Drew mystery instead of brushing her teeth, the way my daughter has done.

The downside of any routine is that it tends toward the tedious unless it is re-enlivened. As dads we have to be sensitive to this. Around the age of eight or nine we should take a look at the routine we have established and see if it needs to be renewed and re-enlivened. Little touches can make a difference. Bubbles for the bath, warm pajamas, a cup of tea before bed—all these things can add an element of newness to a ritual that is starting to be the same old thing. Also, adjusting the bedtime so that an older child stays up a little later than younger siblings, finding a more grown-up story to read, or allowing for a quiet time in bed with the light on can help children understand that their father is aware that they are getting older. Being older means having certain privileges, but it also means being more responsible. Children like this trade-off.

If we enable our children to become more responsible in the bedtime process, we have made an important transition. Through our active and emotional involvement we have helped our children become more independent. And still, we are not yet home free. With the onset of adolescence and the teenage years, outright resistance to any routine can occur. The bedtime routine has certainly changed over the years, and the parent no longer puts the teenager to bed nor wonders when the young person disappears into the bathroom for extended periods of time. And there will be times when our kids will just resist sleep. We will hear, "Why do I have to go to bed now?" "My friends don't go to bed so early," and "All of my friends stay up until 11:00 on school nights." At this stage our children are going to ask that our primary involvement with them regarding bedtime be on a thinking level. They will be extremely sensitive and often unreceptive to our response. We will be called on to state our case clearly and in a most dispassionate way.

These discussions will intensify through high school, and even our most cogent arguments will be rebutted and dismissed. Make no mistake: Children want to argue. They need to exercise their thinking, and this is how they flex those muscles. It is their way of utilizing and developing the third aspect of their three-dimensional nature, thoughtful engagement, and it is also how they establish their independence. Their opinions may seem extreme and deliberately provocative, and yet they should receive serious consideration. We should engage our children in these debates, but never insist on agreement. However, on a personal level we should always insist on a courteous interchange. Our children want to know where we stand, and we should make that clear on three levels. Through our thoughtful explanations we clearly state what we believe. Through our heartfelt love we make it clear that we care more about our children than about any disagreement. And last, we calmly tell them in a firm and pleasant way what we expect them to do. "Please turn the radio off." "Please head off to your room." "And please remember that in a year and a half when you are in college, you will be able to stay up as late as you want and I will never know."

In order for this to work, we must be comfortable with the idea of being an authority. Many fathers struggle with this notion. Sometimes this struggle is a reaction to being raised by an overly authoritarian father. In other instances it grows out of a concern that a father's love and affection for his children will be obscured if he assumes this role. At other times fathers sense that being an authority is inappropriate with very young, imitative children and that it is counterproductive and sometimes destructive with teenagers. All of these are valid reasons for wariness. And yet the fact is that our children need *both* fathers and mothers to be authorities, but they need us to apply this role at the right time and to conceive of this role in a new way.

In those first seven years of childhood our primary response needs to be active. Young children need to be diverted and redirected more than confronted. Knowing this will help fathers avoid a protracted battle of wills or a tedious parental lecture. Young children are easily distracted. If we present them with another activity, or move them away from a difficulty to another situation, we can often defuse a potentially explosive situation. To do this we will need to be alert, ready to act, and attuned to the situation so that we can intuitively sense, like a manager knowing the right moment to remove a pitcher—when things are about to deteriorate.

Working with first-graders has given me the opportunity to observe many children at this critical juncture. Seeing children in the context of a larger group allows the overall pattern of child development to become apparent. For instance, most children's eagerness to imitate diminishes as they enter grade school. Children sense this on an unconscious level. The word *copycat* becomes a derisive term in the early grades. Even children's games reveal this movement away from imitation. The popular early-grade game, "Simon Says," is a case in point. If you simply imitate, you lose. Instead you must wait for the authorized command, "Simon Says, hands on heads." This type of authorized command is present in "Mother May I" and "Red Rover" as well. It is easy to see that the free and spontaneous play of early childhood now begins to give way to games with rules and rituals. The children are feeling their way into an age of authority.

Although children need a portion of authority at all ages, it is primarily in the second phase of childhood when parental authority plays its most significant role. In this second stage of child-hood, our children will come to understand that we authorize many things that they can and cannot do, so they will ask permis-sion. For the seven- and eight-year-old in particular, what parents say is generally beyond questioning. "My mother says..." and "My father says..." are so often heard. Our children should accept us as authorities because they love us, not because they fear us.

*Authority* is one of the most misunderstood terms. We often miss the obvious connection between *authority* and words like *authentic* and *author*. If we are to be authorities in the best sense of the word, we must be authentic. This means that we must strive to understand how we want to be as fathers. We must become comfortable in the best sense of the word, comfortable with who we are and happy with how we interact with our chil-dren. We must develop our own understanding of the interplay between structure and freedom, between formality and informal-ity, so that we don't discipline our children according to someone else's standard for proper behavior, but rather our own. We must strive for the ease that arises at those special times when our true self shines through. When we are authentic, we can be the right kind of authority.

When seen in this light, it becomes clear that being an authority is much more of a creative undertaking than usually imagined. Once we sense how it is that we want to be with our chil-dren, it then becomes our task to work with our wives to create a home environment that allows this to take place. This is where both fathers and mothers become authors. We begin to script our family life in order to allow what we value to come forward.

For example, my wife and I value family time and especially the interactions that take place around the dinner table. Having dinner together is not easy in these busy times, and it was difficult for us when our boys were in high school. They both played on the basketball team and often would not arrive home at night until around 7:00 p.m. Our daughter, who was around two at the time, ended up eating dinner and going to bed much later than we would have liked, and yet we chose this scenario so that she could eat with her brothers. We valued this time together and felt that as the authors of our lifestyle this was the script we wanted. It was worth the extra effort. If we had asked our teenagers if they wanted to come straight home after a game or practice, they would have probably said no, that we shouldn't bother to wait and that they could eat leftovers or, better yet, stop and get something on the way home. But as the adults, we felt that it was our responsibility to direct and author the family life. Now, when we look back, we are all glad that we did.

Scripting your family lifestyle is done on both small and large levels. It can determine how you spend the weekend, how you celebrate a holiday or a birthday, how you spend your vacation, or how you share household responsibilities. But the more you feel your way into the role of being an author, the more creative your fathering becomes and the more you enliven and lighten the word *authority*.

## PREDICTING DISCIPLINARY SITUATIONS

The smooth stretches of childhood may lull us to sleep. Sooner or later our children will try the squeeze play. It will be at these times, when we least expect it and are most vulnerable, that our children will surprise us with their misbehavior. Caught off guard and overwhelmed, we will be more likely to overreact, to hurry our throw, to make the impulsive, but not the smart, decision.

We should also remember what we were like as children. It is always helpful to recall some of the things we did as kids that we hoped our parents would not discover. We should assume that our children will do at least some of the same. We should even try to predict the areas where transgressions will occur.

During the middle years children often play outside with friends after school or on weekends. They will either come in at a certain time or we will call them. We should anticipate the day when they will decide to come in late. Of course, it will probably be a day when we have somewhere to go and everything is a bit rushed. We will call, call again, and still get no response. We will hope for our child's imminent arrival, only to be disappointed again. If we can muster the patience, this is the perfect teaching opportunity, and one where it may be necessary to say, "We will speak about this later."

So much of what we do in the early years with our children concerns the formation of habits. We have looked at the importance of establishing good habits, but we should be equally diligent in avoiding bad habits. We should avoid the habit of calling our children repeatedly, because by doing so we are encouraging them not to respond. We should certainly not look the other way when they disregard the parameters we have established. School-age children are fascinated with the game "Truth, Dare, Consequences," just as we probably were. This game can serve as a reminder to us that our children want consequences for their actions, not lectures. These consequences, however, need to be based in understanding, fairness, and creativity if they are to be most effective.

A sense of humor, often the hardest attribute to maintain in a disciplinary situation, can serve us well. Tardy children could be required to check in every fifteen minutes the next couple of times they are out playing. With a watch to guide them, better still with the timer alarm set, they will need to interrupt their play at frequent intervals to come to the door and check in. Each time we can express our great delight at seeing them, letting them know that we would like nothing better than to have this pleasure continue on a regular basis if they chose to come home late again.

Responding to problem situations in the right way during the extended journey that is child rearing can be the biggest challenge for fathers. It is often the area that will require us to work most strongly on ourselves. Each of us has our strength, that area where we are above average; but that strength has within it an inherent weakness.

For example, if you are a father with boundless energy and staying power, you are a doer, quick to act. This strength will allow you to spontaneously take on great projects with your children without fear or hesitation. Your energy level will be comparable to your children's, and you will be able to participate in much of what they do. However, in a disciplinary situation, especially with older children, this strength, if unchecked, will not serve you well. You will often regret a quick, spontaneous, energetic response to misbehavior, because by its very nature it lacks reserve and circumspection, thoughtfulness, and even tact.

A thoughtful, observant father will be aware of the subtleties and nuances of his child's behavior and the complexity of each situation. He will be keenly attentive and perceptive. But this tendency toward reflection, if unmediated, will cause difficulties for this father, especially while his children are young. His inclination will be to observe rather than act decisively, and will cause his responses to disciplinary situations to be late and less effective. Similarly, if an emotionally involved father responds emotionally to a difficult situation, it will often create more problems. It is important for all of us to look at the way that we meet difficult situations and find out how our response can be prompt, thoughtful, and at the same time sensitive.

## THE IMPORTANCE OF SELF-DISCIPLINE

The story is told that Mahatma Gandhi was once approached by a mother who had an unusual request concerning her boy, who had a special problem. It seems that the child had a difficulty controlling his consumption of sugar and the mother asked Gandhi to speak with the boy and get him to stop. Gandhi agreed, but days passed and still no conversation had taken place. After a week or so, the mother went to Gandhi and expressed her disappointment that nothing had transpired. Gandhi's reply was that before he could speak to the child, he himself had to stop eating sugar.

For words like discipline and authority to lose their stigma, we must recognize that what is required is, first and foremost, self-discipline on the part of the father. Fathers who wish to guide their children will have to take themselves in hand. This can be the most arduous task.

We must come to see that what we call misbehavior on the part of our children is often connected to our own shortcomings. If our children are impulsive or moody, quick to anger or slow to get started, we need to look first at ourselves. When we encounter our children's most intractable behavior, there is a good chance that it has come from us. As much as we would like to attribute these shortcomings to our wife, or at least to her family, there is an equal likelihood that we are responsible. If our children's behavior is particularly irksome, then it is probably striking close to home. There is perhaps nothing so distressing as the sense that our children exhibit the very character flaws that we have been trying so hard to conceal. We feel found out, and this is a humbling experience.

This was particularly hard for me when I watched as one of my sons stumbled through his first two years at college. His poor class selections and dropped courses, his ignored syllabi and low grades were like a video replay of my own poor start in higher education.

The recognition that our problems have become our children's problems, despite our best intentions, is painful. This also occurs when a father who has a tendency toward procrastination watches as his own child leaves a large homework assignment to the last minute and then begins to sink under the weight of having so much work to do in so short a time.

Seeing our faults so clearly and then sensing that others see them as well is not necessarily an experience that is detrimental to parenting. Rather, this experience gives us a more valid assessment of ourselves and can leave us open-minded, unassuming, and willing to learn. If we are now able, because of our love for our children, to focus our efforts on working on ourselves, we gain the ability to help our children overcome their problems. This work opens us to the highest in ourselves. John Gardner alluded to this in his book, *Youth Longs to Know*:

> Self-improvement for the sake of others is creative in the truest sense of the word. By bringing to ascendancy in ourselves that supernatural power that makes mere men and women into true human beings, we add to the sum of existence. This power brings new things to pass, both in and through us. Just as the sunlight streaming through the window rejoices not only the one who opened the shutters but everyone in the room, so also the creative power of the spirit is by no means restricted to the individual who summons it.

Changing ourselves for the sake of another is undeniably a spiritual act.

## WORK BOTH SIDES OF THE PLATE

◆

SWITCH-HITTERS AND COMPLETE PITCHERS
HAVE THE EDGE IN ANY SITUATION THEY
FACE BECAUSE THEY HAVE OVERCOME ONE-
SIDEDNESS. THE ABILITY TO TEAM UP WITH
YOUR SPOUSE HELPS IN THE SAME WAY. IT
CAN AFFORD FLEXIBILITY AND SUPPORT,
BUT IT CAN ONLY BE ACHIEVED THROUGH
PATIENCE AND PRACTICE.

When I am coaching, I often tell my players, especially my infielders and my catcher, "Be quick, but take your time." I had read that this was what John Wooden told his basketball players at UCLA, and in a surprising way these two contradictory statements make perfect sense, especially in pressure-filled situations. Co-parenting will also require that we make sense of ostensibly opposing points of view.

Imagine that it is Sunday evening and the day has already been too long. You have just spent the afternoon taking the children to see their grandparents, and it was not a perfect visit. Your older daughter was out of sorts, so quarrelsome that even the smallest matter became an issue. She ate too many sweets, interrupted the adults, and could not be pleased or placated. She was complaining and stubborn, in spite of the fact that she had been given special treatment, the kind of special treatment that only grandparents can give.

For one reason or another, dinner ran late, good-byes took longer than usual, and now you are arriving home later than expected. You have just walked in the door, your wife has taken your youngest child, the one who fell asleep in the car, upstairs when suddenly the phone rings. You turn to pick up the phone, but before you do, you face your oldest child, the one who has been fussy all day, and you offer her a chance for a little redemption. You tell her clearly that she should go and put on her pajamas and wash up and brush her teeth.

After speaking on the phone for a few minutes, you continue to unpack the car when you realize that you haven't heard anything from your daughter for a while. As you walk toward the bedroom all is quiet. Not a sound is coming from your child's room, and for a second you indulge yourself and imagine that she has actually put herself to bed.

As you turn the knob on the door, you are unprepared for what awaits you. There is your daughter reclining across the bed, one pant leg off, one still around the ankle. Her shirt is on but her shoes are thrown here and there, and she is looking at a book. You are pushed to the brink. What have you managed to convey to this child? She is ungrateful, ill-mannered, and uncooperative. Trying to rein in your rising anger, you take her by the arm, not so gently, and you march her off to the bathroom, barking one-word directives through clenched teeth: Wash..., Brush..., Pajamas!... When your child is finally in bed, you stagger to the living room and collapse on the couch. Your wife arrives and you are ready to commiserate. Hearing your wife begin with an incontestable statement, "What an awful day," you are primed to join in. Fueled by frustration, you take a stronger position than usual. "You're damn right, it was awful," you say. "Could you believe how our daughter acted, constantly whining and complaining?" "I was never so embarrassed." "What have we been doing wrong?" "Something's got to change."

Somewhat surprised by the strength of your words, your wife starts to modify her position. "Oh, she wasn't that bad," she begins, but before long, the conversation shifts, and your wife adds, "How else could a young child behave in a situation like that—too much sugar, too much television, too much adult conversation. Any child would act out." You remark that it makes no sense to make excuses for the child. "Out in the real world, no one will make excuses for her. Do you want to enable her? Regardless of what is going on, she should know how to behave."

When your wife responds, it is now no longer a matter of what your child needs to learn, but rather a question of what you need to learn. "How can you expect your daughter to behave when she's had all that soda and candy? Why weren't you watching her, anyway?" or "How do you expect a child to act when she has been inside all day?" And last, "Why did you have to spend all day watching that stupid game?" Suddenly, a bad day has gotten much worse. The conversation has hit bottom and you are both furious, absolutely certain that the other is wrong.

Oddly enough, it would be just as easy to conclude that both parents are right, or at least primarily right. One parent feels that the environment determines the way the child behaves. The other parent believes that the child needs to learn to act properly regardless of the environment. Both positions make sense. The answer rests somewhere in between these two opposing points of view, but where? There is no one answer. That is what makes parenting such a challenge. The right response is different for each family, and, for that reason, parenting is much more of an artistic, creative process than we usually suppose. There are no easy answers when solutions require the balancing of two opposing points of view.

## WORKING TOGETHER—
## THE YIN AND YANG OF PARENTING

Making the most of opposites is important work. This is what good pitchers, like Greg Maddux, do exceedingly well. Inside, outside, up and down, using all of the strike zone and continually changing speeds. Parenting as a couple is similar.

When placed in close and continuous proximity, any couple will develop diverging points of view. Perhaps this is our way of achieving balance. If our partner is in favor of order and predictability, we will discover a new appreciation for spontaneity. If our partner can see the positive in any situation, we develop an affinity for realism. If our spouse is goal oriented, a take-charge person who can get the job done, we suddenly see the value in living in the moment and enjoying process. This is part of our human condition, an innate sense that balance is essential.

Given this dynamic, which occurs even in the very best relationships, parents are as likely as anyone to end up in polarized situations. In order to keep from growing further and further apart, husbands and wives need to find common ground. An essential question that fathers and mothers often need to answer is, "Are we talking about the same child?" If we base our understanding on a common picture of child development and developmental needs, we will be better able to answer this question in a compatible way and unite our efforts for our child's benefit. This united effort will make all the difference. If we look at our child's misbehavior in the light of the paradigm in chapter two, we will be able to ask key questions: Was there any purposeful activity for the young child to imitate? Was there quiet downtime as well as more exuberant time for expansive and expressive play? Were our teenagers engaged in the thoughtful, mature conversation and included in the adult responsibilities? If we have confidence that our children's needs are being met, then we can have certain expectations for their behavior without feeling that we are being unreasonable. Talking about these expectations is not always easy, but it is nearly impossible when the children are around.

My wife and I run each morning. We don't run very far, but we do it regularly. We have found that this is one of the few times when we can have an uninterrupted conversation. It is true that there have been occasions when we weren't speaking to each other by the last lap, but most often we have been able to talk about important matters, especially matters concerning the children.

Evenings are also a good time to speak. I am of the mind that regular, early bedtimes for children are important for parents as well. It is essential that we have some quiet evening time together to reflect and to speak about our parenting concerns. If we find time for these conversations in the normal schedule of the week, we will be able to enjoy ourselves and speak about matters unrelated to the children when we go out for dinner or to a movie.

It is good to remember that what we share, above all, is a desire to do what is best for our children. We must work together to create a unified picture of what this is and then support each other's efforts in making it happen.

### FINDING OUR COMPLEMENT

I have tremendous confidence in fathers. The dads that I have met are hard working, caring, humorous, insightful, and above all deeply committed to their children. And yet, even the best dad can raise the level of his game. Every strength has its implicit weakness. If you are a good fastball hitter, your instantaneous response and the speed of your bat make you susceptible to the change-up. Good hitters have to become complete hitters.

In a good marriage you won't find the duplication of your strengths, but rather the completion. Your partner's personality, her understanding, and her abilities will complement yours. This is part of what you sensed when you found her so attractive and surprising when you first met. This complementarity is also what makes your wife important to you as a father. She has the ability to further your understanding of your children and to make you a more effective parent.

I have always loved playing with my children, especially when they were really young. I was never shy about sitting down on the floor and setting out the tracks for the wooden trains or building with blocks. I enjoyed joining in, and I thought that my children enjoyed my joining in as well. We would build elaborate buildings and intricate track arrangements and then act out the loading and unloading of the train cars. In the end there would be grand set-ups, but it was basically my doing. What my wife showed me was that this play wasn't always best for the children because it was too much about me. My children also needed self-directed play where their imagination and associations had free rein and where all I did was observe from a distance. Uninter-rupted play offers children important advantages. Through this free play, children become more independent, and creative forms of play evolve. Although it took awhile, I came to see that for young children, play is their work. And like us they need focus more than distraction. My wife taught me that there are certain occasions when I should resist the temptation to get down and play like a child—when it is really better for the child to continue to play alone in a concentrated manner.

Another area in which I learned a great deal from my wife

was that of *style*—that it is not just what you do that is important, but also how you do it. When my wife and I first met, I was a single dad with two sons, ages nine and five. On our first date we went to see a play and then came back to the house to relieve the baby-sitter and to have a cup of tea. I would never have characterized my house as a "guy's house," but this night I saw it through new eyes. When I went to make the tea, I realized that I had no teapot. Nor did I have one of those nice little honey jars—just a big quart jar. The overhead light in the kitchen suddenly seemed so bright that when I looked at the walls in the kitchen and in the hallway, I saw all the dirty fingerprints that I had never noticed before. It was as though my awareness had increased, and I was not happy to see my house in this new way. Needless to say, things changed.

On a mundane, but nonetheless important, level, lunches also became more attractive. Thinking about the lunches that I used to make I am reminded of the statement by the writer Anne Lamott: "In general, come to think of it, when fathers made lunches, things turned out badly. Fathers were so oblivious back then. They were like foreigners." My sons still joke about the fact that my lunches could be so predictable. Cheese sandwiches, fruit, and far too many nuts and raisins became the staple of the lunch boxes, day in and day out. I figured if you had a good thing going, you stayed with it.

Marriage too, is a path of self-development. When we undertake parenting and marriage at the same time, the challenges increase exponentially; we are placed in an emotional crucible. Our former life, the life before children, which was once orderly and comfortable, is now being heated and refined, and what is being distilled and extracted is selflessness. Just look at how the lifestyles of your friends who don't have children proceed in a strikingly carefree way. Their activities and interests at home have undergone small changes, while your life has gone through astounding and sometimes shocking changes. The combination of parenting and marriage demands our very best. The secret is that our very best isn't just in us; it is also kept and protected by our spouses.

In my early years as a teacher I often wondered what it meant to "love" my students. I felt that this was something I should do, but I didn't always know exactly how. Then one day I had a parent conference for a difficult child. I was describing the difficulties to the mother in an extended fashion. The child was disruptive in class; his work was sloppy; his assignments were incomplete; and his homework was turned in sporadically. "Yes, I know," the mother said, a little discouraged. Then suddenly she brightened and added with a smile, "But isn't he a remarkably lively boy." This was the perfect example of a mother's love. Regardless of the difficulties, she could still see the child's best. I realized then that faithfully maintaining a sense of what is best in another is an important part of what it means to love.

I have always felt that I was a capable and decent father, but the truth is that my wife has made me better. It makes all the difference how our actions are viewed in the home. When they are seen with love it is easier to be a good father. It's like playing in front of a home crowd. But when our behavior is seen critically, through the lens of "There you go again" or "You always do that," it leaves us leading with the wrong foot, and everything we do seems wrong and out of step. And make no mistake, children are extremely sensitive to these undercurrents. A wife's love is a great gift to us, both as men and as fathers. It sustains us in challenging parenting situations by helping us to be more natural and at ease—in short, to be more authentically ourselves.

This isn't to say that my wife is always complimentary. However, I nearly always feel that her criticism is constructive. It contains an implicit "You're better than that," and that is empowering. There have been numerous times when my wife's support has helped me through an emotional logjam. Once after a regrettable argument with my then-teenage son, an argument that had him marching off to his bedroom and slamming his door and left me fuming at the dining room table, she simply said after awhile, "You don't want to leave it like that. Why don't you go and speak to him?" This was exactly what I wanted to do, but emotionally I was stuck. It is especially in the area of emotional interactions that my wife's advice has helped to complete and enhance what I had to offer. This ability to see a partner's very best, to see who the other person really longs to be, is a treasure.

Marriage is about creating this treasure and then maintaining and protecting it. It is far too easy to squander this gift through thoughtless and unfeeling actions. The same three capacities for active, emotional, and thoughtful involvement that enhance your interactions with your children will be significant in your relationship with your wife and will help to preserve the love that is so easily obscured by the cares and endless responsibilities of parenting. What we do, even the little things, will matter to our wives, as will our thoughtfulness, interest, and attention. But as with our children, what we feel and how we express it may matter most.

## IF YOU HAVE A SHALLOW BENCH, KEEP YOUR GAME SIMPLE

◆

PARENTING ALONE IS ONE OF THE HARD-
EST THINGS A FATHER CAN DO. WHEN YOU
DON'T HAVE A PARTNER TO TURN TO, KEEP
YOUR GAME SIMPLE AND DIRECT TO AVOID
SERIOUS ERRORS (AND TO KEEP YOUR
SANITY).

As difficult as it seems to parent together, it is even harder to parent alone. Being a single dad was not something I envisioned when I started out as a father. In fact, I was married for nearly ten years before the bottom suddenly fell out. Having marriage problems forced me to encounter the unthinkable. I thought I was the perfect family man—and I was wrong. Suddenly, I came to see myself as a middle-aged guy, balding and physically unfit, with an extensive list of inadequacies—and I must admit that the case against me was not without merit.

The prospects of being an ex-husband brought me face to face with a variety of fears. I was afraid that I was going to be alone, but more than that, alone with two children who would keep me busy every moment that I wasn't working. I also was afraid that everything I had built my life on was somehow flawed. I had carried around this complimentary picture of myself as a good husband and a good father, and suddenly it was being called into question in a most startling way.

I responded, once I got over being completely stunned, by trying to look at myself objectively, through the eyes of another, and then by working harder to fix the problems. If I had settled into a dull and predictable routine, I would change. If my life was too fixed, plodding, and planned, I would be more spontaneous. If I was too quick to speak, I would learn to listen. In short, I was committed to do whatever it took to make my marriage work. The odd thing was that in spite of my efforts, I felt I was building with sand. Everything kept slipping away.

I am such a private person that it was impossible for me to tell anyone about what I was going through. I could not express the pain and uncertainty that I was experiencing to friends, not even to my own brother when he came for a visit. One day, however, I did mention to a long-time colleague of mine at work that I was having problems in my marriage. I knew that he and his wife had their own challenges, and I thought that his experiences might be helpful. I hinted at situations I wouldn't describe. I alluded to my struggles without sharing too much. And yet, even with the little information I gave him, his advice was both surprising and appropriate. "Sometimes," he said, "you just have to let go." That was when I began to see that there was a side to me that I had never developed. I had never learned to let go, to release my hold and to see what was meant to happen.

Just about that time I had a dream that a friend and I were in a rowboat on a lake, and we had fallen overboard. This was a vivid dream at a time in my life when my emotional travails were causing me to dream constantly, partly because I was sleeping so poorly. In this dream both he and I were sinking in water that was well over our heads, and we were struggling to swim back up. We were making little progress, as there seemed to be some force pushing us down. Suddenly a strong voice said to relax and sink, and hit bottom. As I woke, I understood that hitting bottom would provide the firm place I needed to push against to get back to the surface.

I know that I am not alone in saying that I learned more in the time that it took for my marriage to break up than at any other comparable period of time in my adult life. This was a crash course in self-development, and the changes were taking place on a deep, structural level, accompanied by loss of appetite, loss of sleep, and loss of a sense of self.

In the end I was left with only the inner core of who I was. The façade, the false pretensions, the overinflated ego were all stripped away. I felt newly defined and refined, and overwhelmingly certain that I was not alone. When all the dust had settled and it was clear that my marriage was over, I was left with a distinct sense of spiritual protection. If I were to put into words what I learned in those nine months, it would be almost exactly like this statement of Rudolf Steiner's:

> Everything of the old must be driven into oblivion. Clouds will gather and man will have to find a total sense of freedom out of the abyss. The human being will have to find all his strength out of nothingness. Outer need will be transformed into an inner need of the soul, and out of this profound anguish inner perception will be born.
>
> We must eradicate from the soul all fear and terror of what comes out of the future. We must acquire serenity in all feelings and sensations about the future. We must look forward with absolute equanimity to everything that may come, and we must think only that whatever comes is given to us by world direction full of wisdom.

After nine months of hell, a new sense of myself was born and I was sure that I was now happy with who I was, and I was not leaving my children.

## STAYING AHEAD IN THE COUNT

Finding myself with a completely new set of responsibilities helped to take my mind off of my problems. When the new school year started I was ready to work, and I was busier than ever. Not only were there students to teach and lessons to prepare, but now there were my two boys to raise, meals to cook, clothes to wash, food to buy, and little time to rest or to feel sorry for myself.

This dramatic change in lifestyle called for a new approach. I felt like a pitcher who had lost a key pitch. I needed to focus and simplify, and to lead with my strengths. In those first few weeks I tried to stay ahead in the count at all times, establishing a sense of order and regularity. The basic essentials—clean clothes, good food, and regular bedtime—were particularly important. We ate at home on school nights, avoiding the easy route of pizza or McDonald's, and I became adept at preparing meals that could be cooked quickly with a limited number of pots or pans. Chili, gumbo, pasta with tomato sauce, pasta with cheese, pasta with white sauce—pasta with anything—became regular meals on our table. But my sons' favorite was kielbasa, sauerkraut, and Rice-a-Roni, which we ate regularly once a week, on the day we shopped. Nearly twenty years later, we still talk about it.

We didn't eat healthily, and our nitrate intake jumped during those first few months, but this was just a temporary blip on the screen. There were a number of compromises that I allowed myself to make. Corn (sometimes in the form of corn chips) would count as a vegetable with any meal. Laundry would not need to be sorted. And I didn't have to clean behind furniture, only in front of it. I promised myself that I would not be fixated on particulars and also that I wouldn't worry about money during that first year. If I indulged in some deficit spending, I would just have to view that money as funds provided for disaster relief.

Within weeks we had established our rhythm, and our life had an air of normalcy. Monday afternoon was laundry time; Wednesday was for shopping; Friday was special; and Saturday morning was for cleaning. Establishing a rhythm is so important for children, as it makes their lives predictable and gives them a sense of security. As a single dad this became my first objective: to make my children feel secure and establish an atmosphere of normalcy.

Single parenting also has its array of opposing tendencies that need to be balanced. As essential as the everyday, customary routine was, so too was it essential to create a sense of newness, making a break with the past and giving the clear impression that we were moving on. With this in mind I changed banks, found a new supermarket, and took my sons to a different swimming pool. I rearranged the furniture, got a new rug, acquired a wood stove, and painted the kitchen. After months of confusion and emotional upheaval, I felt that I was once again able to take charge of my life, and that feeling was exhilarating.

I see now that there was a tremendous infusion of energy into my life as a response to this personal crisis. The crisis turned out to be a creative force, and, looking back, I am so glad that I didn't squander it. The time following the breakup of my first marriage became one of the most creative periods of my life.

At the suggestion of a good friend, I enrolled in an art course on Sunday mornings, during the time when my children would visit their mother. Through this course I rekindled my interest in calligraphy, an activity that proved to be both calming and creative. I became intrigued with ancient Celtic writing, and by the end of the course I was even able to produce a Gaelic verse, which I had printed as a Christmas card. I sent it to my friends to let them know that I was doing better than I ever expected.

A new abundance of quiet evenings provided time for more than just calligraphy. I began to write during this period and, in spite of the busyness of my schedule, published a number of articles on education in the course of that year. I also took a mime class with another good friend, making the best use of the time I had for myself, treating it like the luxury that it was. I sensed that I should try everything that interested me. Fear of failure no longer seemed so important.

In considering past events, I can see that these creative outlets opened for me because of the emotional turmoil I experienced. My crisis was also my opportunity, as it stirred up intense feelings and by doing that enabled me to be more emotionally active than I had been in a long a time. Being more active on a feeling level led to a new affinity and appreciation for art, for nature, and, most of all, for friends and family.

As much as I thought that I was standing on my own feet at the time, I now see clearly that a silent network of support embraced me and that I wouldn't have managed well without this help. It seemed that each Friday, my sons and I would receive a dinner invitation from parents at our school. It took me a few weeks to realize that this was a quiet conspiracy to keep us well fed and to give me a break at the end of a long week. On weekends when the boys were with their mother, I got calls from friends to go out to the movies, or dancing, or white-water rafting. Close friends offered to watch my sons and constantly made their offers of help known. I was learning how to accept the help of others—and that is a lesson that comes slowly for many men.

Times of crisis let you know who you can count on, and my parents were there, as they always had been, willing to help in whatever way they could. I had spent years in rebellion, vowing that I would be different than my parents, but I came to see most clearly that their constant support and unqualified love were something upon which I couldn't improve. I saw then that if I were going to be a good father, I would have to be there for my children in the same way for an unbelievably long period of time.

## Being There for Our Children

The work schedule can be one of the greatest hindrances to effective fathering. I was amazed when we began our fathers' group sessions to see how many men would arrive at our 8:00 p.m. meetings in their suits, having come straight from work. All fathers need time to be with their children, but for single dads this is even more crucial. There will be surprise illnesses, dental check-ups, parent-teacher conferences, as well as school performances and games. This is also our work.

I realized then how fortunate my situation was that I could spend so much time with my children. My work as a teacher allowed me to be available to my children continuously. Because I worked at the school that my sons attended, I took them with me to work each morning and brought them home at the end of the day. If there was a medical emergency at school, I was only a few steps away. If school was closed for snow or opening two hours late, it was not a problem. Our holidays, half days, and vacations coincided, and I knew their friends and their teachers, and consequently I knew exactly how they were doing during this period of adjustment. Although I took work home with me on most evenings, I rarely, if ever, had to ask permission from my boss to have the evening off to see my children in a sporting event or school play.

Although teaching is not a lucrative profession, it allowed me to exchange money for time, and time is something we desperately need to be good fathers. Today so many men feel compelled to work ten- or even twelve-hour days or to travel extensively. These fathers feel torn between their desire to spend more time with their families and their need to provide financially. In his book *Fathering,* Will Glennon relates a conversation he had with a father who was struggling with his work schedule:

> I worked with this man who had no life whatsoever except for work.... He'd be on the telephone at eleven o'clock at night, thinking he was just incredibly important. One evening I was getting ready to leave, and he was needling me about "commitment" and "dedication"; I told him about a quote I had read somewhere, something to the effect that on their death bed very few people ever complain that they wished they had spent more time at the office.

Although we all can't be teachers, single fathers need to have flexible schedules, schedules that allow them to be with their children for significant amounts of time at both ends of the day. It is helpful that the times in which we live allow us more options with our work arrangements. With the advent of personal computers and the Internet, more and more fathers are able to work at home. And yet, at the same time, there is a greater demand on working men to put in increasingly long hours on the job and to travel extensively. When our work schedules and parenting schedules collide, we experience incredible pressure and stress. Any unexpected variation in our elaborate and precarious arrangements and our house of cards can collapse, leaving us distracted and agitated. All working parents experience this upset periodically. A single parent's experience is more frequent and more dramatic.

## Staying Calm

Because our children are closely connected to our emotional life, our stress and strain and our moods in times of pressure will strongly affect theirs. Especially for single parents, our emotional state matters, and sometimes that is harder to control because the pressures are that much greater and we have little or no support. We need to shield our children during these difficult situations. One time when children are extremely vulnerable is during interactions with our estranged or ex-spouse. Emotional upset can easily flare up during the transfer of children during child visits. We need to safeguard our children by tempering our emotions, knowing that what we experience during these difficulties is conveyed to them through visible and invisible lines of communication.

The transition that takes place before and after a child visit is a difficult time for everyone. Our children are moving from one emotional environment to another, and they often feel conflicted and at loose ends. To ease this transition, it can be helpful to find a ritual of activity that is done as part of the adjustment process. It became a regular occurrence in our home to bake muffins when my sons would return from their visit to their mother's. My youngest son, for whom this transition seemed the most problematic, would be the baker, an activity he has always enjoyed. Before he arrived home, the bowls would be out on the counter with the recipe and the necessary ingredients. He would get right to work and mix up the batter, fill the muffin tins, and put them in the oven, and by the time they were finished baking he seemed more himself. Nothing needed to be said. He was pleased, and we had muffins to go with the soup that we ate for dinner on those nights.

## MOVING ON

During the breakup, separation, and divorce, I learned a lot about myself, but also a good deal about the kind of person that I was best suited to be with. Just by considering all that I had been through, I became conscious of the fact that I liked a woman to be strong, independent, active, and funny. I liked a woman with strong feelings, but not one so sensitive that a misplaced remark would ruin the day. I needed a woman with a good temper, as it made me feel amazingly calm, as well as someone who understood how good Brooks Robinson was and what it meant to hit to the opposite field. The big question was, how would I find her?

In general, it seems much easier for a single dad to meet someone who would be interested in an instant family than for a single mom. A single dad also has the advantage of coming across as a nurturing male, and that is definitely a plus in the eyes of most women. But even in the best of circumstances it is amazingly difficult to meet the right person. I knew that my only hope was to keep my eyes wide open, to listen carefully, to stay out of bed—which would only confuse matters more—and not to worry about being alone. I was given another opportunity to practice letting go and putting my trust in whatever comes.

Oddly enough, the first time that I went out with my second wife I had no idea that I was out with the very woman I was hoping to meet. It was a nice enough evening, but at certain moments during the date I found myself thinking, "Good woman, but we wouldn't get along." Mostly I thought this after she started defending my ex-wife, but I figured we could try again. The second time I asked her out, she cancelled. A few months later we struck up a conversation and made plans to go out, but she backed out again. I started to worry that I was this bothersome guy who just wasn't getting the message, so I gave it up. About a month later she asked me out. From that point on things picked up.

Fortunately for both of us, Carol had made plans to study in England and would be away for the summer. This time apart, a little more than seven weeks, was probably just what we both needed. It gave us the opportunity to see if there was a genuine connection between us. It also gave me time to clear my head and think about how this new relationship would affect my children. The time apart wasn't easy, but it was helpful. When Carol returned to the States, it was clear that we were interested in continuing this new relationship. It was time to include the children.

When school began that September, we started to do things together. Outdoor outings provided a good opportunity for Carol to get to know my sons. We went hiking, rowing, and berry picking, and we traveled to New York City to visit my family for Columbus Day and Thanksgiving. Carol added an important dimension to our family, but it wasn't always easy. Being with children on a more continuous basis was new to her, and the boys and I had ways of doing things that weren't always so appealing. That first year was certainly a period of adjustment.

Some aspects of divorce just aren't easy. Sharing the children can be hard, even for the custodial parent. Being at a school event or a sporting event and having your children come with your ex and then leave without you takes getting used to. You feel incomplete. Yet remarrying and bringing a new person into the family also has its share of difficulties that can test all involved in new and surprising ways. Even in a fairly amicable situation, divorce is hard, harder than I ever imagined.

It is important to keep in mind that the same three-dimensional framework that works for fathers also works well for blended families. Start out with activities that appeal to the children. In our case, we took full advantage of the outdoors. We camped, went to the beach, just did unusual and special activities whenever we could. If it was possible to coordinate our outdoor events with good food, we did that, too. We had bike trips that passed by really good ice cream shops. We concluded day hikes at restaurants with great pizza or at cafes with hot drinks and desserts. If we found that an outing worked particularly well, we did it again around the same time each year, and it would help us establish milestones.

To form emotional bonds, we established rhythms and traditions during those first years together. Like authors, we got to decide the way we would now celebrate a birthday, a special holiday, or the end of school. We sought for situations where the emotional climate was joyful and relaxed. That first year, on the last day of school we went out to a local farm and picked strawberries. We stood in a large open field, and the cares of the year started to fall away as the promise of summer stretched before us. We ate and picked and ate some more. My sons have now graduated from college and moved away, but we still pick strawberries on the last day of the school year with our daughter—same farm, same farmer, and still a great way to mark the end of the school year.

Above all, there is a need for thoughtful attention to recognize those moments when the awkwardness of this new arrangement makes the children feel uneasy. We also need to be aware when an occasion or a remark brings up tender memories. The more conscious we are of these situations, the less painful they will be.

I certainly didn't do everything right as a single father, but I gave it my best, and I look back over those days with a certain fondness. Those times helped me to form a deep connection with my sons and led me to a new life. Being a single parent wasn't the easiest situation, but I am sure it had the most to teach. It taught me what a gift it is to have a companion to parent with and how this relationship can be supportive and stimulating physically, emotionally, and mentally. In the end, I learned to relax and to be upheld by my new wife, by friends and family, but mostly by that numinous presence that gives meaning to even the most difficult circumstances.

Like all parents, I worried from time to time that separation, divorce, and remarriage had taken their toll on my children. A couple of years ago our oldest son met a lovely divorced woman with a young child of her own. When he first told us of the seriousness of this relationship, we felt that we needed to caution him about the complexities of this type of family situation, to let him know from our experience just how challenging it could be. "You know," we said, "this won't be easy. It will be complicated and stressful, and these complications won't go away for years." "Oh," he replied, "I didn't think it was so bad. Besides you both were a great example of how this could be done." The compliment was secondary; the fact that he felt good about the way he was raised was of primary importance. He and this young woman were married last year in a lovely ceremony that was designed to include their little boy. Like millions of young people, he had grown up with divorce. Like countless other adults, he and his new wife were committed to restoring and reforming a family, definitely a worthy undertaking.

## DEVELOP WELL-ROUNDED PLAYERS

◆

COMPLETE PLAYERS WHO CAN HIT FOR AVER-
AGE AND HIT FOR POWER, WHO CAN RUN THE
BASES WITH SPEED AND PLAY DEFENSE,
ARE SOUGHT AFTER BY ALL TEAMS. WELL-
ROUNDEDNESS COUNTS IN CHILDREN,
TOO. LEARN TO HELP YOURS DEVELOP THE
SKILLS THEY NEED TO BE ALL-AROUND
HEALTHY, BALANCED INDIVIDUALS.

It happens every spring. The baseball season starts and I find myself coaching our high school team. I stand on the infield hitting grounders and throwing batting practice and feeling extremely fortunate to pass a warm, sunny afternoon in such a pleasant way. However, after an initial practice or two, I begin to experience another feeling, one brought on by the overwhelming complexity of this simple game. Baseball teams need so much to develop properly: They need practice for cutoffs, rundowns, pickoffs, steals, bunts, fake bunts, defensive rotations. The list seems endless, and each item requires its own set of fairly particular arrangements. One thing we know is that good teams, teams that are well coached, have been organized to meet those needs.

Our children's lists of needs are just as long as an entire team's. When we attempt to meet those needs, we immediately sense that our work as fathers can be just as overwhelming as any coach's. We, too, need some way to organize our efforts and this is where our three-level paradigm can serve most effectively. Of course, any conceptualizing about life has its limitations. Children develop differently and manifest their individualities in different ways. In order for our paradigm to serve us, especially when we seek to meet the specific needs our children, it must be fluid and alive, not cut and dried.

In trying to present this paradigm as clearly as possible, I have focused primarily on the three ways in which we need to relate to our children and in which our children relate to the world—through activity, through feelings, and through thinking. In addition, I have tried to show how childhood itself is divided into phases and how each phase has its most pronounced need. The young child up to age seven longs for activity; the school age child from seven to around fourteen is especially attuned to emotions; and the teenager during the third phase is keenly interested in thoughts and ideas. The way that these three aspects manifest themselves varies with each child. Some children are always active, while others respond emotionally regardless of their age. And of course there are children who are attentive, thoughtful, and alert from the time they are little.

Upon closer investigation, we see that this paradigm is more complex. Each phase of childhood has all three aspects blended together in varying proportions depending on the age and disposition of the child. If we explore this matter more fully, we will be able to see how these three general needs weave together in specific needs.

## THE NEEDS OF THE YOUNG CHILD

I can still remember my parents packing the car for our summer vacation. The trunk of our '52 Ford was filled to capacity with suitcases and boxes of food. The back seat belonged to my brother and me and we were told in no uncertain terms that we had better behave. "You are going to be in the car for a long time. Bring some-thing to play with and don't fight. This will be a long trip."

That "long trip" was a fifty-mile drive that we made once a year to stay at a little motel on a small lake on Long Island. Nowa-days this distance is a daily commute. Back then, during most months, I wouldn't be in the car for two hours. Yesterday alone, my daughter was in the car nearly twice that long when we took her brother to the airport and then drove to visit her grandpar-ents. Each day she is in a vehicle for about an hour just going to and from school. She spends at least twenty-five hours a month in a car without any special trips. In just forty years this aspect of family life has changed dramatically.

Our times are skewed away from activity, especially sponta-neous outdoor activity. The vast majority of children spend more time sitting inside cars or in the house than playing outside. Skip-ping, hopping, and running have been relegated to games classes, and many school districts have canceled these classes to allow for extra academic lessons. Our children need to be robust and vital, and they are being deprived in this regard today. Modern children need more active time outdoors, where they can climb trees and fences and explore both their environs and their abilities. This is remedial work for our kids, and fathers need to be their advocates in this area so that children can regain the physical vitality, the ability, and the agility that children had in years gone by. If our children today are wired and wound up, it is often because they have been denied the remedy for their nervous energy. Our chil-dren need large-muscle activities like the ones used when playing tag or hide-and-seek, the kind needed for riding a bike, jumping rope, playing ball, skating, or simply walking.

The first step a father can take in this direction is to take his children outside at an early age. After six weeks, children can regularly spend time outside regardless of the season. If children are dressed properly and the weather is not severe, this outdoor time will pave the way for greater physical resilience.

During the first spring after my daughter was born, my wife ordered a "baby sling," a carrier designed to support a newborn child as if she were held in your arms. This carrier was a gift for the whole family. I could come home after work and use it to take my daughter for a walk. This gave my wife some time by herself and gave me an opportunity to be out in the fresh air with my daughter after being inside most of the day. I could look down and see my daughter's face as we walked. I could talk to her and sing to her. She could look up and see my face, which was becoming more familiar, or look past me and sense the wind in the trees and hear the occasional bird sing.

This routine evolved as the months passed. She gradually outgrew the baby sling, and we graduated to the backpack and then eventually to walks together. Each of these routines helped to establish my connection with my daughter and laid the groundwork for all that we would do together outdoors as she grew older.

A good deal of the time that I spent actively involved with my children out of doors centered on chores. Although I would not, as a rule, run errands with my children, I would be eager to have their company when I worked in the yard. There is no end to the work that needs to be done around the house on a weekend. Each season has its own demands. Usually there are certain chores that I avoid and others that are more agreeable. The gutters are always waiting for my attention, and my lawn is neither the shortest nor the greenest on our street. But I have a woodpile that I do not avoid. I am fascinated by the sound of a maul striking a log. We heat our house with wood, and I can wax enthusiastic over the qualities of ash, oak, and locust. I've spent a lot of time gathering, sawing, splitting, and stacking wood with my children.

On many Saturdays when my daughter was young, I would head out to the yard with my second cup of coffee and begin my work. Within five or ten minutes the door would open and my daughter, who was four or five at the time, would come out. She would find a safe place, not too close, and begin to play. Within a few minutes she would go back inside and reemerge with her toy telephone and a pencil and a pad of paper. As I continued to split wood, she would start to play. Her toy phone would ring (her sound effects) and she would answer, "Country Wood Shop." Then there would be a pause as she allowed time to listen to the imaginary voice on the other line and then she would say, "Yes, we have oak and cherry and some poplar. Would you like ten pieces? Yes, we deliver." This was a girl whose mother had her office in our house and who had grown up in the era of mail-order catalogues. She was imitating conversations she had heard from both ends, and her phone etiquette was well developed. She would then make some marks on the paper that were meant to resemble writing, and then her phone would ring again. All the while I would split and stack the wood. She would ask me questions from time to time. "Do we have any maple today?" If I said yes, she would tell the imaginary customer we did and then "write" down another order.

As I split wood seriously, my daughter would keep playing. Sometimes she would wander off to dig in the yard, and I was always aware of where she was. We were outside like this in all sorts of weather. My primary aim was to spend time outside with her and provide an example of purposeful activity and, of course, to get some work done. While I was doing this, I got a memorable glimpse into my daughter's world and split and stacked my wood as well.

Doing things with our children does more than simply satisfy the need to be active. The time we spend with our children helps to form our emotional connection with them and becomes part of the foundation of their emotional security. And when our regular interactions with our children are imbued with love and affirmation, we give them an even richer fabric of emotional stability. When I meet adults who have grown up without a father's presence, I begin to sense the true value of what we often take for granted.

The activities that we do with our children will also provide rich learning experiences. Fathers should encourage their children to follow their interests through curious and investigative play and through healthy interactions. If we are there to converse with our children, to read to them, to show an interest in what they do, and to listen to their questions, we will be able to trust that their natural intelligence will develop properly on its own.

Young children don't need information as much as they need imaginative answers to their questions. When young children ask an ostensibly scientific question, they may not want a factual answer. For instance, a young child may ask, "Why do stones fall?" Our inclination might be to begin by mentioning gravity and then move on to the rotation of the Earth and centripetal force. If we do, our children's eyes will probably glaze over. British educator A. C. Harwood suggests that it might be more appropriate to tell a young child that rocks fall because they want to go back to the Earth, which is their home. That kind of answer makes more sense to a young child.

Our children often ask direct questions, but they don't always want direct answers. One second-grader I taught years ago came up to me at the start of school and asked, "Why are there different bathrooms for boys and girls?" I expected older children to ask me questions pertaining to sex education, but this second grader caught me off guard. I was at a loss, so I did what I was trained to do in such situations—I asked her the same question. "Why do you think boys and girls have different bathrooms?" "So we don't get confused," she replied, and then skipped off. I had been beginning to wonder whether I needed to head to the library to get a book to see how others explain the anatomical difference between boys and girls to children. That seven-year-old neither wanted nor needed such an answer. Now, you might think that a more scientifically minded child would not have been satisfied by that conversation, but the student that I mentioned is now a medical doctor.

It is especially with factual questions that we need to find a way to our child's heart. If our child asks, "What is the Sun?" we may be inclined to turn to our encyclopedia program. There we are likely to come upon a description that runs something like the following: The sun is merely a ball of exploding gases, ninety-three million miles from the Earth. It is a great nuclear reactor producing temperatures in excess of...etc. From an emotional perspective, this statement isn't true at all. The sun isn't *merely* anything. It is absolutely central to our experience of life. It affects our moods, our health, our environment, our economy. It is the alpha and the omega of each day. Fathers face the challenge of finding answers for their children's questions that satisfy them on all levels and help them feel at home on this Earth.

## THE NEEDS OF THE CHILD IN THE MIDDLE INNINGS

We need to recognize that anything that our children do, especially in the middle innings of childhood, is permeated with elements of emotion and thought. Whether our children are playing baseball or violin, they will be engaged emotionally and thought-fully. We have to keep this in mind when we try to determine what activities are best during this middle period of childhood.

The need for activity spans all the phases of childhood. When the spontaneous play of the young child begins to give way to the organized and ritualized play of the grade-school child, fathers often consider organized sports as an option. Organized sports and sports classes, however, are not usually well suited for young children. Although they do provide outlets of vigorous activity for rambunctious children, they have too many restrictions and requirements. Besides, the skill level of most young children is such that the players often spend most of the time standing around. For seven- and eight-year-olds, a Little League baseball team will offer only a fraction of the activity of an infor-mal game in the backyard or in the park where a child can come to bat three times in an inning, not just in a whole game. Little League baseball is often reduced to a lot of sitting for long, tedious walk- and error-filled innings and a lot of standing around. A healthy young child's tendency during these periods of inactivity is to find something else to play with, whether on the bench, at second base, or in right field. This is a normal response, but it is not always well received.

A child's first sports experiences are best had around the home. This nonthreatening environment provides the right atmosphere for the mastery of new skills at a leisurely rate, and a good age to begin is around seven. In this informal setting, chil-dren feel free to be more imaginative, and imagination is such an important part of play at that age. If we could watch and listen to children without being seen while they play, we would hear how they talk to themselves the way we once did, announcing the var-ious plays of the game. They will imitate the gestures and the mannerisms of their favorite players. They will sense when their swing feels like Ken Griffey, Jr.'s; they will feel when the dip of their shoulder is the same as Mike Mussina's. Children's hearts play an important role in their sports experiences. They open their hearts to their sports heroes and to their fellow players. This happens readily in the safe confines of the backyard or on the neighborhood street.

When it comes time to put a child on a team, somewhere around the age of nine, the coach may be the single most important factor. The coach will set the tone for the interactions of the players, their sense of teamwork, the seriousness of their effort, and their attitude toward their opponents. There is a fine line that we must walk with sports, a delicate question of balance. Children should try hard to do their best, to come to practice regularly and to games. But before adolescence they don't need to be made to feel that the outcome of any one game is too important. Even after adolescence, it is the coach's job to keep things in perspective, and good coaches in high school and college do this. Often, to ensure that this happens, committed fathers end up volunteering themselves to coach.

Many fathers worry that starting children in organized sports at a later age might jeopardize their athletic development, but I don't believe that is true. Children often learn more creative abilities with informal sports arrangements and less perfect equipment. A good example of this was the soccer star Pele. As a child, Pele had only a large ball of paper wrapped in tape that he would dribble barefoot through the crowded streets of his Brazilian city, weaving in and out of crowds. This kind of practice prepared him to react instantly to defenders far better than dribbling through a sequence of stationary orange plastic cones.

Sports are a truly modern phenomenon. We could alter the

Dickensian phrase slightly and say "They are the best of activities; they are the worst of activities." From a positive perspective, sports promote teamwork and perseverance. They help children to grow stronger and to become more agile, teaching them at the same time to overcome adversity and to accept defeat with dignity. At their worst, sports expose children to unrealistic salaries and unrealistic goals, flawed role models, excessive competitiveness, and a distorted view of the human body. Clearly, they are a double-edged sword, which means that fathers need to approach sports with their eyes wide open. If our children participate in organized sports, we must look for other influences to help guard against one-sidedness.

Years ago, Willie Gault, a track star and a wide receiver for the Chicago Bears, danced with the Chicago ballet; it made national news. The American public was duly impressed that an athlete could have artistic sensitivity as well as physical prowess. Former presidential candidate Bill Bradley is another example of a well-rounded individual. He was a star basketball player for the New York Knicks championship team and also a Rhodes scholar. Many people were impressed that someone so accomplished in sports could also be keenly intelligent and thoughtful. We innately sense that balancing physical ability with emotional sensitivity and thoughtfulness is admirable, but not the norm in sports. How then do we bring this experience into balance for our children?

My second son was a very good baseball player in both high school and college. One of the reasons he was so good was because he had an intense dedication that caused him to have either a bat or a ball in his hand all the time. It was clear that, left to his own devices, he would dedicate every waking moment to baseball. It was also clear to me as his father that this would not necessarily be in his best interest, because other sides of his personality, other abilities, would be neglected. Because he loved music and loved to sing, music lessons seemed like a good idea. Little did I know when he started these lessons, right around the age when he joined his first baseball team, that they would complement his sports development perfectly by encouraging a whole different side of his nature, one even more strongly linked to his feelings.

Music, like baseball, requires developed muscle memory. In the same way that a player fields hundreds of ground balls until it becomes second nature, a musician plays the scales again and again until the fingers move automatically. The difference was that the muscles needed to play the viola were primarily small muscles, those that assist more delicate and precise movements. Playing a musical instrument led my athletic child in a wholly new direction where exacting, careful movements were needed rather than force and strength. My son, who did not like precision, whether it had to do with handwriting or drawing or spelling, was now asked to work on a side of himself that he would have rather left undeveloped. This made him a more complete person in the end.

Playing a musical instrument requires that children work with all three of their capacities, and that is why it is so valuable. Children need to be alert and attentive to every sharp and flat, the key signature, their posture, the fingerings, all the details. They have to learn to be sensitive to the music, to their sound, and to the sound of others with whom they might play. Music lessons also require tremendous dedication and discipline. The daily practices strengthen a parent's will as well as a child's. But in the end the child will have a tremendous gift—the ability to play, and perhaps create, music.

Music speaks to the inner child. So do drawing, painting, and drama. But perhaps the most direct route to a child's heart is through a story. People from all cultures have understood this for generations.

Recently, I watched *Field of Dreams* and was amazed at how much this movie was about fathering. I watched with appreciation as Kevin Costner regaled his "daughter" with stories of Shoeless Joe Jackson. These stories answered her questions and at the same time touched her heart by planting the seeds for her future appreciation for one of the game's truly exceptional players. They were told in a delightfully casual way and had wonderful appeal. This movie served as clear reminder that children need stories at all ages for their emotional development—and, of course, not just baseball stories.

Story time should be a regular event for families. It encourages closeness, both physical and emotional. Many fathers share stories from their childhood or make up stories for their children, sensing that a simple story of everyday events is basically what a young child needs.

Young children love stories, and this love will continue as they learn to read on their own and move away from picture books to more complex and lengthy tales. Fathers need to become part of story time early on so they can be regular participants when the need for stories is greatest in the middle years.

One summer on a trip to Pennsylvania, we stopped at a roadside stand and my daughter came face to face with an Amish girl a little older than she was. As we were driving off my daughter saw this little girl running barefoot across a field with her little brother and their pony. From that moment on she was filled with questions. These questions gave rise to simple stories about this little girl, whom I called "Yonnie." In my ignorance I chose a name that sounded authentically Amish but turned out to be an Amish boy's name. Fortunately, my daughter never knew. The stories that I made up detailed all the simple seasonal chores that Yonnie would do with her father—pressing cider, plowing the fields, loading the horse-drawn wagon, and driving it back to the house or to the market. Each and every story would end with a bountiful Amish meal and then with Yonnie being carried to bed by her father. For over a year my daughter repeatedly asked for Yonnie stories and of course, to be carried to bed like Yonnie.

Simple and lovely picture books will also find favor with young children, and local libraries today have an ample supply. Children will often request the same book again and again. Favorite stories will be like family friends. *Tikki, Tikki, Tembo; The Pasta Pot; Fin M'Coul;* and *Grandfather Twilight* were all favorites at our house.

As our children grew older, longer read-aloud books became popular. Shortly before bedtime we would turn off the ringer on our phone, turn down the lights, and gather around the fire for stories. Each good book was like a dessert to be savored as long as possible. We read some great books over the years (The Chronicles of Narnia by C.S. Lewis, *The Princess and the Goblin* by George MacDonald, *Watership Down* by Richard Adams, and most recently, the Harry Potter stories by J. K. Rowling). It was a sad day when our sons reached an age when they thought they were too old for stories that were read aloud.

In the late seventies I saw an article in *Readers Digest* entitled "Thank You, OPEC." The article was about the adjustment a family had to make during the oil embargo and the subsequent fuel shortage. The author's family had installed a wood stove and found that their hearth became the focal point of their family's activity. They no longer sat in front of the television at night; instead they gathered around the fire and read. The author wrote that although the energy crisis had produced outer hardships, it provided rich inner rewards.

As our children grow older, their inner life will develop

breadth and depth. There will be a growing part of them that is private, in some cases secret. It is in this region that our children will begin their search for meaning. This search may cause them to ask profound questions, questions of a religious nature. Although these questions will probably surprise us and perhaps make us a little uneasy, they will be important and should be answered with great care. This could mean that we have to ask our children to wait a day or two while we consider the question and the answer that we wish to give.

If children are not discouraged in this way of thinking, they will be naturally religious. Their early experience in life closely parallels the opening lines in William Wordsworth's poem "Intimations of Immortality from Recollections of Early Childhood":

> There was a time when meadow, grove and stream,
> The earth, and every common sight,
> To me did seem
> Appareled in celestial light,
> The glory and freshness of a dream.

And yet as children grow older these intimations and connections begin to fade and in their absence can rise longing and questions of a religious nature. The word *religious*, which comes from the Latin root *religare* (*ligare* gives us the word *ligament*), basically means reconnected. Fathers who wish to meet this need for their children may find this the most challenging task of all.

Organized religion does not always provide what children need, which is a quiet, nondogmatic sense that they are drawing closer to a great and mysterious Presence. Children achieve this sense more readily through mood and story than through sermons. If we can find or create the right kind of religious celebration for our children, we can facilitate a religious mood, one sustained through inner calm and outer stillness. This experience can take place in our home as well as in a place of worship. It can take place perfectly in nature, especially at sunrise or sunset. But if we wish our children to attend a traditional religious ceremony, that ceremony should be brief. If there is subtle lighting and singing, a child's soul will open readily. Then with the right story, and most of all, the right attitude, our children's need for meaning will be met on this most significant level as well.

## THE NEEDS OF TEENAGERS

Don't make the first or last out of an inning at third base. Don't try to pull an outside pitch. Don't walk the first batter of an inning. Don't overthrow. Don't intentionally walk the potential winning run. The list goes on. Baseball definitely has its set of "don'ts" and they are an important part of an understanding of the game. I have tried to stress the positive aspects of fathering in *Covering Home*, to focus on what *to do* with our children rather than what *not to do*. When it comes to raising teenagers, a different approach is probably in order. Perhaps this is the time to look at a few "don'ts" for fathers of teenagers in an effort to uncover one essential need that young people have in the late innings of childhood, and that is the need to understand that life is a two-way street.

Several months ago, I was speaking with a group of parents in Canada and we somehow found ourselves considering the topic of home construction and teenagers. Partly in jest, I suggested the following: Don't buy a really good dishwasher for your kitchen. Don't put a phone jack in your child's room. Don't buy a house with a bathroom for everyone. These suggestions had one common thread. They all would give rise to situations in which teenagers would have to cooperate with others and, on occasion, put their needs second.

It's not just the dishwasher that prevents young people from actively helping around the house. It is also the busyness of their schedules and ours. However, it is critical that teenagers learn to accept responsibility, first at home and then in the workplace. When we look for a way to encourage our teenagers' need to be active, we should consider their need to work. The lessons that young people learn from a summer or part-time job are significant. A job will enable them to understand the value of money, to learn self-discipline, and to come to a sense of their own growing ability. It will afford them the deep and lasting satisfaction that comes from an experience of self-sufficiency. A summer job will give structure to their free time and put them on a healthy summer schedule. It is clear that teenagers are happy when they are active in many ways, but working outside the home is one of the best.

The suggestion that young people not have telephones in their room stems from the sense of how isolated we can be in our own homes. Whether it's the telephone, the television, or the personal computer, it is just unfortunate when our children retreat behind closed doors at times of leisure and avoid contact with their family. In contrast, sharing a couch, a newspaper, or a conversation helps to develop important social skills. Young people who regularly sit down and converse with their family are bound to acquire emotional sensitivity, tact, and sympathy.

In addition, learning to share a bathroom provides valuable experiences. Over time it will help teenagers to speak up for themselves without getting upset and to develop the reflex of thinking of others. By learning to pick up a wet towel, lower the toilet seat, and remove the hair in the bathtub drain, they will be moving toward emotional maturity. This process will make them better roommates in college, better housemates after college, and when the time comes, better partners.

Perhaps you can see how these seemingly minor suggestions can assist us in meeting the one pervasive need that our teenagers have—the need to be less self-centered. We see this desire for selflessness in their commitment to causes. Animal rights, human rights, concern for the environment, concern for the homeless and the hungry—these are ideas that many young people take seriously without a single thought for personal gain. When given the opportunity, they will express these thoughts in surprising ways. Many parents are eager to discuss these and other matters with their children. The fact is, however, that we will probably learn the most about what our children think when we hear them converse with others.

The families of teenagers that work the best usually have an open door to their house (and refrigerator). A free flow of young people, friends, family, and neighbors fosters the kind of stimulating atmosphere that helps teenagers feel at ease and open up. Through the conversations that arise naturally, through both speaking and listening, young people will explore what they think. When conversations take place in an air of openness and interest, young people will feel fulfilled on this important level. In this most vital way their need for thoughtfulness will be met through conversation and dialogue. It is evident that what teenagers need, a sense that life is a two-way street, is fostered and encouraged by their strong desire to think. Young people really are interested in what others think (parents excepted, of course). The traffic of these ideas is so important to them.

The three elements of our paradigm can be seen in the needs of our children through all three stages of development.

When we examine our children's specific needs, we will see that they are founded on our children's continual need to be actively, emotionally, and thoughtfully engaged. The proportions will change over time, but the three-dimensional paradigm will remain. This is the essential idea that can help us achieve a better understanding of what our children need from us over the course of their childhood.

## REMEMBER,
## YOU CAN'T WIN THEM ALL

◆

FAILURE IS AN INTEGRAL PART OF BOTH
BASEBALL AND FATHERING. THE IMPORTANT
QUESTION IS NOT HOW TO AVOID FAILURE
BUT RATHER HOW TO RESPOND TO IT.

One holiday weekend when we were in New York visiting my family, my son and daughter were in the dining room conversing and commiserating when my mother asked somewhat impatiently from the kitchen why the table was still not cleared of papers and set. Without missing a beat they both answered simultaneously, "It's dad's fault." It was my stuff on the table, but I had only just walked in the room.

This situation is not unusual. Fathers often take the blame. The family's official scorekeepers are continually posting a large "E." Sometimes we don't deserve it, sometimes we do. Both in baseball and at home, when errors are made, they are noticed, and someone is always keeping score.

Fathering and baseball are closely linked through this notion of failure. The names of Ralph Branca, Bill Buckner, and Mickey Owen, not to mention the Mighty Casey, stand out in stark relief in baseball lore, not because they were good ballplayers, which they were, but because they failed memorably. Great hitters like Willie Mays and Stan Musial, who have earned their way into the Hall of Fame, still failed to get a hit in two out of every three official at bats. Even the world champion Yankees lost sixty times in 1999. In baseball as in fathering, failure is a given. The most important question is not "How do we avoid failure?" It is rather "How do we minimize failure?" and, just as crucial, "What do we do after we fail?"

## GOING OVER OUR OWN SCOUTING REPORT

My experience has shown that it is extraordinarily difficult to see ourselves objectively, to view our actions with the same dispassionate, critical awareness with which we view others. It is easy to delude ourselves, to make allowances and excuses. Yet it is not helpful to do this when our actions, our emotional responses, and our thoughtlessness have caused problems. At these times it is important that we try to see ourselves as others see us when they recognize our shortcomings. This can be painful work. We will be embarrassed by these realizations, sometimes ashamed, and invariably humbled, but always better off. These realizations will break up the logjam of self-assurance that prevents us from changing dramatically. The necessary first response to failure is to read our own scouting report and seek what is so elusive: true self-knowledge.

At times of failure, our quest for self-knowledge will focus on our weaknesses. Careful reflection will be done either on our own or, in more severe instances, with the support of family counseling. Through this reflection we will most likely come to see that the type of situations that present problems for us today are similar to those that have troubled us over the years. These difficulties rise out of our human nature and our natural shortcomings. There are two very different ways that we should approach our shortcomings: as *pragmatists* and as *idealists*.

## THE PRACTICAL FATHER

As pragmatists we have to take a careful look at the problems that arise. We have to examine these difficult situations to see if there are common elements in them. It's not a bad idea to write the situations down and then begin to look at them closely. When do the difficulties arise? What is happening at the time? Is it a time of stress for the parents? Is it a time of transition (coats, boots, hats, mittens, car seat, stroller, backpack, etc.)? Or is it a situation where we are applying some external pressure (for instance, trying to hurry our children along to school)? Do the difficulties occur just before dinner when everyone is hungry and a little irritable? Do they occur on Saturday morning when the children seem at loose ends because there is plenty of time, but little routine? We can pose these and more questions as we look for patterns. Recognizing in advance that certain times are problematic can be a tremendous help. It allows us to be mindful and to make the necessary adjustments.

When my son attended the school where I taught, he would sometimes come to my classroom at 3:00 with elaborate plans for his afternoon. He was often keen on going home with someone in his class or going off to watch one of the sports teams play and wanted me to pick him up somewhere across town at a certain time. I was usually more than a little distracted at dismissal time with parent conversations, exiting students, and a classroom that needed some attention, and he was usually in a hurry to get the okay for his plans. In short, we were headed for a disagreement. Once I realized how regularly we argued when this situation arose, I saw that he needed to make such requests in advance. If he wanted to visit a friend, he could not ask me for the first time at 3:00 on that very day and expect "yes" for an answer. This became one of our team rules, and once it was in place, afternoon arrangements were less problematic.

In other situations we may find that predictable responses, not surprises, give rise to the difficulties. Our children may feel that our first response to every request is, "No!" Or they may feel that our most commonly used phrase is "Not now." As our children grow older we will be able to detect in their expressions the disappointment that arises from our typical response.

Over time our children will know us all too well. They will be able to predict our response to a multitude of situations with amazing accuracy. And they will know every possible way to provoke us. Once we become conscious of this, however, minor adjustments on our part can make a world of difference. If we anticipate the challenging situations and keep in mind that our children can be just as predictable as we are, we can surprise our family with our unexpected responses, particularly humorous ones, and these surprises can help everyone, especially us, get out of a rut.

We also need to probe our likes and dislikes to see what circumstances trigger our mood changes and then, most important, ask ourselves why. Is the upsetting situation one that we can help to rectify? Is it a situation that we need to learn to accept? Or is it one that we should simply avoid?

Fathers need to know their limitations. There are times when it is legitimate and necessary to create buffer zones. Sometimes siblings just have to argue, and there are instances when it is better for us just to go outside and find something to do. A good friend's daughters were home recently from college and they were arguing at length. I noticed one morning that their dad washed all of his family's vehicles, even his daughters'. That was how he kept his sanity. Although we shouldn't habitually avoid challenging situations or leave our wife to do the hard work of damage control, there are times when we simply need to look the other way. As my children grew older, I reminded myself more frequently that I could not fight every battle or solve every problem.

## THE IDEAL FATHER

Although pragmatism has its advantages, it cannot, on its own account, transform our fathering. The pragmatic father needs the uplifting impulse that comes from continually striving for the ideal. There is always a discrepancy between the fathers we want to be and the fathers we are. If we commit ourselves to trying to become ideal fathers, we unlock creative power. Our striving, more than our actual success, is the important factor. This intangible and unnoticeable work, this inner effort, will be conveyed to our children through unseen connections. Our failure, if met with our best effort, can become the pearl that grows in response to an irritating grain of sand.

It is unrealistic to hold out hope of becoming the ideal father. But *trying* to become the ideal father is valuable work, work we can all undertake. This doesn't mean that we no longer make mistakes. Rather, it means that we try extremely hard not to make the same mistake twice, or three times, or more.

Sometimes, however, one mistake is enough to do significant harm. Anger, yelling, and most regrettably, hitting, can leave us feeling that we have done irreparable damage to our children. There *will* be times when our effort to engage our children in a three-dimensional way proves insufficient, when our lack of resolve, sensitivity, and thoughtfulness causes us to fail.

The best way to break out of these slumps is to return to the basics and double our efforts. A determined push to improve is the first step. Our three-dimensional paradigm will guide us in assessing our actions and interactions. Our continual resolve to reverse troubling trends is essential: Remember, good hitters hit well with two strikes.

And yet, I have found that in spite of my sincere and determined efforts, there are still more times than I would care to mention when I continue to fail. There are challenges in parenting that exceed those of the game of baseball. After all, our children have something unique in them that we cannot fathom, and this slowly emerging self often makes them unyielding and unpredictable. This, in turn, can give rise to unpredictable, unyielding, and extremely unsatisfying behavior on our part. At moments like these, when I am convinced that I am ill suited and undeserving of the love of my children, I turn to prayer. And in that prayer I ask for help to be a better father and to heal the wound that I have caused. I have never felt that my prayers have gone unanswered.

As parents, our capacity for regret is immense. We feel badly when our actions fall short and we feel badly when our children's actions fall short. When our children are intractable despite our best efforts, we also blame ourselves. It is legitimate to ask for more insight, more patience, some new understanding of our children that will enable us to unravel the mystery of who they are and what they long for from us.

If we seriously take up the task of *trying* to become ideal fathers, we will need to set aside five or ten minutes at the start or finish of each day. At this time we can take stock of how we are doing as fathers, read something inspiring, and remember our resolutions for improving our interactions with our children. We must always be mindful of our resolutions, our promises to ourselves. Perhaps we can see as well that each failure holds within it the potential for positive growth and change. And changing for the better is the greatest gift we can give to our children. This is expressed poignantly in the book, *Turning*, by an anonymous author:

> The greatest single thing that you can do for your children is to work on yourself.... Even as characteristics are handed down from one generation to the next and you become conscious of them, so may the noble thought *I shall transform this in myself* also be handed down.

I have always admired players who resurrect their careers, like Steve Carlton, Andres Galarraga, Dennis Eckersley, and even Mark McGwire—players who seem to have two smaller careers contained within their successful long careers. When McGwire came up to the Oakland A's in 1987, he had outstanding season, hitting forty-nine home runs and winning the Rookie of the Year award. He became the first player to hit more than thirty home runs in each of his first four seasons. But by 1991, McGwire's batting average had dropped to .201 and his home run total to twenty-two. There were serious questions about his future in baseball. During his phenomenal, seventy-home-run season in 1998, few remembered that McGwire had gone through the eye of the needle and transformed his career. His early years were built primarily on natural talent; the astounding part of his career, the later years, were built on overcoming and transforming natural weaknesses. As fathers we are called to improve in the same way, not for a long-term contract or for fame, but simply for the good of our children.

## START A LEAGUE OF YOUR OWN

◆

TEAMWORK CAN BE ONE OF THE MOST
IMPORTANT INGREDIENTS OF GOOD FATHER-
ING. FINDING OTHER FATHERS WITH WHOM
TO TEAM UP CAN GIVE US THE ENCOUR-
AGEMENT AND FELLOWSHIP THAT WE NEED.

I hope that *Covering Home* has enthused you about the prospects
of fathering, for it is indeed true that we have the possibility of
making a significant difference in our children's lives. Even
though all fathers encounter difficulties, this possibility of
making a difference is within the reach of all dads, especially if we
work as a team. The numerous challenges of fatherhood diminish
when we are able to work together with other fathers. Therefore,
the next logical question should be, "How do I start a fathers'
group in my community?"

Although a fathers' group can start in a home, it is probably
better to begin in a central location. A school, a neighborhood
community center, or a faith-based organization will work well.
After receiving permission to hold the fathers' group, place an
announcement in a community newsletter and put flyers around
the school, church, temple, or local library asking all dads interested in attending to contact you so that you have a clear idea of
how many might attend.

It is important that there be clear time parameters for the
meetings. I would suggest a time limit of an hour and half for

each session and an initial gathering of six or eight sessions. After these initial meetings, I would stop and not meet again for a couple of months. Given the busyness of everyone's life, it seems good to pick definite periods of time for the meetings rather than have a continuous schedule where attendance vacillates as people drop in and out.

You might also note in the announcement that the group will study a book on fathering. Many books would serve this purpose. *Covering Home* would work well, as would *Manhood* by Steve Biddulph or *7 Habits of Highly Effective Families* by Stephen Covey.

Future reading assignments should address the needs of your group. At the very first session of our group I asked the dads what they hoped to gain by participating in our group. They expressed a desire to understand their children better and to know more about their children's education. I looked for readings that would deal with these issues. Because we all sent our children to the same school, our readings pertained to Waldorf education.

Our weekly reading assignments were never too long, usually around fifteen pages, just enough to provide focus for our conversation. Our readings gave us an important anchor and kept us from drifting too far in personal reflections. And yet, as one of the dads said to me recently, "The book is only the vehicle." It takes us to the place where meaningful conversation begins.

With each reading assignment, I asked the fathers to share what they liked and what they didn't and also to raise any questions that they had. My hope was that our conversations would elicit a sense of trust. I wanted the fathers to bring out the questions they carried around but rarely shared.

Because conversation is such an important part of the fathers' group work, the number of participants also matters. Having more than twenty members will make it difficult for everyone to participate in discussions. I find twelve to eighteen fathers to be a nice size for the group. This provides the critical mass that is needed to give a clear sense of purpose to the meetings and yet still allows important conversations to take place.

To facilitate these conversations, we usually started each session with a check-in, where we would hear each father tell how things had been going in his life since our last meeting. This turned out to be a far more valuable time than I had originally imagined. Usually these check-ins gave rise to parenting questions. Sometimes, however, they revealed unexpected crises. These crises always got everyone's attention and showed the strong sense of community that had developed in a few short weeks.

In addition to the questions that arise in the check-in time and through the reading assignment, the facilitator should pose questions designed to stimulate important conversations. One such question is, "How would your children describe you as a father?"

This is a delicate question because it cuts to the heart of our uncertainty, but it also helps us commit to change, a starting point for most parenting work. Two other important questions are, "What do you remember most strongly from your relationship with your father in a positive way?" and "What do you remember most strongly from your relationship with your father in a negative way?" Both questions elicit so much discussion that they can take a couple of sessions to explore fully. In addition to these topics, our fathers' groups tried to address the following questions: "How can I deal with anger?" and "Why am I starting to sound like my parents?" These questions also led to valuable conversations.

The men in our group sought ways to meet in which conversation was not the main focus. There were weekend basketball games, camping trips, and perhaps best of all, opportunities to work. When we were reaching the end of our first study session and were discussing how we could meet more actively so that we didn't just sit around and talk, there were suggestions for canoe trips and camping trips that were met with scattered enthusiasm. Then one of the fathers spoke up and said that we should work together side by side and bond as men have traditionally bonded. So I mentioned that our school needed a sandbox for the children in the younger grades. One of the fathers said that a club he belonged to had dozens of trees that were blown down in a recent storm and that we could have the logs if we wanted to cut them up and load them on the back of his truck. Another was a landscape architect who volunteered to draw up some plans, which he then brought to our next meeting. It was a beautiful design for an enormous spiral sandbox. The wall of the sandbox would be made of logs of increasing heights, with the highest log, from which children could jump into a large mound of sand, at the center of the spiral.

The Saturday we built the sandbox, more than a dozen fathers showed up with many children and some energetic moms, as well. We dug great trenches, sawed logs to the right length, and then set them into the holes and filled them in until they were quite secure. We worked for the whole day with a strong sense of camaraderie and satisfaction. When we were done, we couldn't have been more pleased. The sandbox was beautiful. The following week a dump truck pulled up at the school. One of the fathers, who ran a construction company, had sent over a load of sand for the new sandbox.

Throughout the eight years since our original fathers' group started, we have reconvened on a number of occasions. Most recently, we started a six-session study group focusing on discipline and the three stages of childhood. This new group was composed of both veteran fathers who had attended the original meetings and dads of young children new to our school. The veteran fathers, who now had adolescent and teenage children, had much guidance to provide for the fathers of younger children. It was great to see that our fathers' group was giving rise to mentoring in our fathering community.

A fathers' group has many benefits to give to its members, not the least of which is the growing sense of fellowship among them. In our group, this fellowship became obvious every evening after our session had ended. I would remain in the classroom where the meeting took place, replace the chairs, close the windows, and make sure that all was in order. I would shut off the lights, lock the doors, and head out into the parking lot ten or fifteen minutes after everyone had left. Invariably, I would see the dads standing by their cars, continuing their conversations and forming new friendships.

To see fathers forming connections with other men reminded me of how much we long for social contact. In too many instances we have lost touch with our good friends from childhood, high school, and college. We have allowed our deep affection for our friends to be buried beneath layers of responsibility and neglected.

In each of our sessions we discovered something in the other fathers that was familiar and common. This gave rise to a sense of common purpose. So many knowing glances were exchanged during our discussions, nods and smiles indicating a deep sympathy and understanding for others. This was just one more of the benefits of having a fathers' group.

Fathers' groups are right on time. In 1994 there were barely 200 fathering programs in the United States. Today, just six years later, there are over 2,000. Last year, the United States Congress passed the Fathers Count Act, providing funding for parenting education for dads. Fathers' groups are a grassroots effort to do this same work. There is a growing awareness everywhere that fathers matter, and this awareness lives most strongly in us. This should be our common bond when we meet in our fathers' groups. We are meeting to support one another in an effort to be the best dads we can for the good of our children and to make the most of this precious opportunity.

## EXTRA INNINGS

◆

*It ain't over 'til it's over.*
—YOGI BERRA

Last summer I was sitting on the beach with my twenty-three-year-old son. He had taken time off from his summer work and his job search and had driven to the ocean to see me. Having graduated from college, he was exploring his options. Reaching into his backpack to take out a book, he turned and asked if I could help him with something. In his hand he held an examination book for a Naval Officers Training Program; it was opened to the math section, where there were quadratic equations, graphs of linear equations, and a slew of signed numbers. "Can you show me how to do this example?" he asked.

I must admit that I had assumed, without a tremendous amount of regret, that my days of helping him with math were over. I laughed to myself to think that he had graduated from college and we still had a chance to meet in this way. That was when I realized once again that there are aspects of parenting that never really end, although they do change, especially when our children head off to college.

Taking my oldest son to college was one of the hardest things I had to do. I remember standing in the parking lot at Guilford College in Greensboro, North Carolina, and feeling my eyes begin to water. My son, sensing this, told us that it would be okay and that he'd be home in just six weeks. But I felt that it would never be the same. He was leaving home and I knew it. During his freshman year he came home regularly—fall break, Christmas, (not spring break—he had baseball practice), and summer. Yet as the years passed he came home less and less, and somewhere along the way it began to feel more as if he was visiting and less as if he was returning home.

I thought it would be easier when his brother went off to school, but it wasn't. There was the same keen sense of loss once again.

Certainly our role changes when our children go to college, graduate, and then live on their own. We hope that they have been well served by our parenting. Rather than seeing them morning and night, if all goes well we may only speak to them by phone every week or two or touch base by e-mail every couple of days. We may help them with taxes, furnish their first apartment with leftover dishes, utensils, and furniture, or help them fly home for a holiday. Little by little, however, we watch as they come to stand completely on their own. Our support and concern are still there, but we have pulled back.

Eventually, there will probably come a day when your child marries, and this too will mark the beginning of another era. There will now be someone in your daughter's or son's life whose concern will be more immediate and constant than yours. This became clear this past fall at my son's wedding. He now had a wife and a three-year-old son, and he was twenty-seven years old. That's how old I was when I was a young father and he was my three-year-old son. We had come full circle. As I watched I was struck by how sweet he was with his little boy. Suddenly, I could sense what Ken Griffey, Sr., must feel when he watches his son play: the deep satisfaction of knowing that the game is being taken to a higher level.

ACKNOWLEDGMENTS

Many individuals helped make *Covering Home* possible.

Many thanks to:

The Michael Foundation for helping to fund this project.

The dedicated members of our fathers' groups, whose stories and insights helped shape the content of this book.

Peter Murdock, Ron Schneebaum, Peter Batzell, Ken Courage, and Jim Hartnett for advice, encouragement, quotations, coffee, and friendship, and for being great dads.

My friends at the Washington Waldorf School for all of the opportunities that this sabbatical year has offered and for my Toshiba laptop.

My publisher and editor, Justin Rood, for asking me to write a book on fathering, working closely with me as it evolved into *Covering Home*, and making it such a gratifying experience.

Writers like Roger Kahn, Roger Angell, Tom Boswell, and Doris Kearns Goodwin, who have shown by example that the subject of baseball can actually raise the level of meaningful discourse.

And last, to Rosemary Petrash, who isn't mentioned often in this book on fathering, but who has always been a key player on my team.